lonely planet

POCKET
FLORENCE
& TUSCANY

TOP EXPERIENCES · LOCAL LIFE

W9-BXT-874

NICOLA WILLIAMS & VIRGINIA MAXWELL

Contents

Plan Your Trip 4

Duomo (p36)
STEVE LOVEGROVE/SHUTTERSTOCK ©

Explore Florence & Tuscany 33

Worth a Trip

Survival Guide 175

Special Features

COVID-19

We have re-checked every business in this book to ensure that it is still open after the COVID-19 outbreak. However, the economic and social impacts of COVID-19 will continue to be felt long after the outbreak has been contained, and many businesses, services and events referenced in this guide may experience ongoing restrictions. Some businesses may be temporarily closed, have changed their opening hours and services, or require bookings; some unfortunately could have closed permanently. We suggest you check with venues before visiting for the latest information.

Florence & Tuscany's Top Experiences

Gaze at the Duomo (p36)

VANIA TONOVA/SHUTTERSTOCK ©

Discover Renaissance Art at the Galleria degli Uffizi (p42)

DETYUNOV SERGEY/SHUTTERSTOCK ©

Explore the Galleria dell' Accademia (p78)

GAID KORNSILAPA/SHUTTERSTOCK ©

Wander the Basilica di Santa Maria Novella (p64)

CELLUOY/SHUTTERSTOCK ©

Learn about Michelangelo at the Museo del Bargello (p102)

ANNA PAKUTINA/SHUTTERSTOCK ©

PHOTOGOLFER/SHUTTERSTOCK ©

Set foot in history at the Palazzo Pitti (p116)

Wonder at the Basilica di Santa Croce (p100)

ISOGOOD_PATRICK/SHUTTERSTOCK ©

ALVARO GERMAN VILELA/SHUTTERSTOCK ©

Marvel at the Opera della Metropolitana di Siena (p156)

Lean in at Piazza dei Miracoli, Pisa (p144)

ROSTY MCELY/SHUTTERSTOCK ©

CRIS FOTO/SHUTTERSTOCK ©

Climb the ramparts of Lucca (p152)

Take a sip in Chianti (p170)

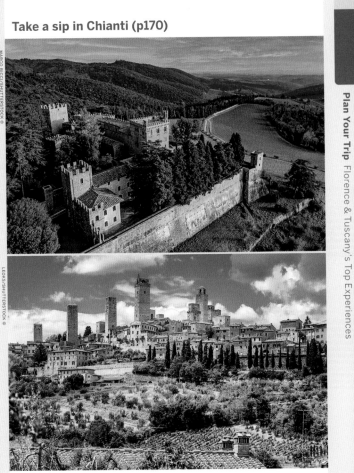

MARCO BICCI/SHUTTERSTOCK ©

LEOKS/SHUTTERSTOCK ©

Explore San Gimignano (p172)

Dining Out

Quality ingredients and simple execution are the hallmarks of Florentine cuisine, climaxing with the bistecca alla fiorentina (pictured), a huge slab of prime T-bone steak rubbed with tangy Tuscan olive oil, seared on the char grill, garnished with salt and pepper and served beautifully al sangue (bloody). Wherever you dine, quality is guaranteed.

Cafes

Florentines don't pause long for *colazione* (breakfast). Most make a quick dash into a bar or cafe for an espresso and *cornetto* (croissant) standing at the bar. At *pranzo* (lunch), busy professionals will sometimes grab a quick snack at a cafe – usually a *panino* (sandwich) or *tramezzini* (the local version of a club sandwich) accompanied by a glass of wine or a coffee.

Trattorie, Osterie & Ristoranti

Champions of traditional Tuscan cuisine, these low-fuss eateries are greatly beloved in Florence. Popular for both *pranzo* and *cena* (dinner), they are often family run and excellent value for money. There's a fine line between an upmarket version of an *osteria* (casual tavern) or trattoria and *ristorante*; service is more formal in *ristoranti* and cuisine is generally more refined.

Enoteche

Enoteche (wine bars) are trending in today's Florence, popular for their focus on quality wine and light, seasonally driven dishes often described as 'Modern Tuscan'. Popular destinations for *aperitivi* (pre-dinner drinks accompanied by cocktail snacks), they are equally alluring for a casual *pranzo* or *cena*.

HLPHOTO/SHUTTERSTOCK ©

Best Traditional Tuscan

Trattoria Mario Sensational Tuscan dining by San Lorenzo market. (p70)

Trattoria Cibrèo Top-notch Tuscan cuisine à la Fabio Picchi in Sant'Ambrogio. (p108)

Trattoria Sergio Gozzi All the classics in an interior unchanged since 1915. (p87)

Osteria Il Buongustai Tasty Tuscan home cooking at a snip of other restaurant prices. (p55)

Best Modern Tuscan

Essenziale Inventive cuisine by one of Florence's most talented chefs. (p132)

Irene Creative bistro fare on Piazza della Repubblica. (p55)

Il Santo Bevitore Long-standing, modern Tuscan favourite on the Oltrarno. (p133)

iO Osteria Personale Creative *osteria* to die for. (p135)

Best Gelato

Gelateria Pasticceria Badiani Handmade gelato and sweet pastries, famed Italy-wide. (p58)

Grom Top-notch gelato near the Duomo. (p56)

Vivoli Vintage fave for coffee, cakes and gelato. (p109)

My Sugar Sensational artisan *gelateria* near Piazza San Marco. (p86)

Best Panini

Semel Creative sandwiches to go in Sant'Ambrogio. (p111)

'Ino Gourmet *panini* near the Uffizi. (p56)

Mariano Favourite for its simplicity, in a 13th-century cellar since the '70s. (p70)

Best Quick Bites

All'Antico Vinaio Mad-busy deli serving iconic cured-meat tasting platters. (p107)

La Toraia Riverside food truck cooking up artisan burgers. (p110)

Trippaio Sergio Pollini Tripe to go in foodie Sant'Ambrogio. (p109)

#Raw Fresh, raw snacks and dishes – all sensational – to eat in or go. (p134)

Bar Open

Florence's drinking scene covers all bases. Be it historical cafes, contemporary cafes with specialist coffee, traditional enoteche (wine bars, which invariably make great eating addresses too), trendy bars with lavish aperitivo buffets, secret speakeasys and edgy cocktail or craft-beer bars, drinking is fun and varied.

Cafes

Florence has cafes of every type – historic, hip, bohemian, cosy and plenty with no frills. Most are bar-cafe hybrids, serving beer, wine and spirits as well as coffee, along with pastries in the morning and *panini* at lunch. Those located on piazzas often have terraces that are perfect places for whiling away an hour or so.

Bars

You can drink at a bar almost any time of the day, but most are at their best from 5pm (aka *aperitivo* time), when many places serve complimentary snacks with drinks. *Apericena*, a brilliant cent-saving trick and trend among students and 20-somethings in Florence, translates as an *aperitivo* buffet so copious it doubles as *cena* (dinner).

Enoteche take pride in their selection of wines and tend to concentrate on Tuscan labels. Most offer *antipasto* platters of cheese, cured meats and crostini (toasts with various toppings) to eat.

Best Cafes

Ditta Artigianale Hipster coffee roastery and gin bar. (p138)

Le Murate Artsy cafe-bar in the city's former jail. (p110)

ELENA KATKOVA/SHUTTERSTOCK ©

Best Wine Bars

Enoteca Pitti Gola e Cantina Serious wine bar opposite Palazzo Pitti. (p139)

Le Volpi e l'Uva First-class food pairings with wines by boutique producers. (p125)

Il Santino Intimate and *aperitivo*-perfect wine bar just across the river. (p138)

Best Cocktails

Mad Souls & Spirits Expertly mixed cocktails in San Frediano. (p137)

Rasputin Late-night cocktails in the secret speakeasy everyone knows about. (p138)

PanicAle Stunning cocktails, craft beer and homemade ginger ale in San Lorenzo. (p89)

Best Summer Terraces

Santarosa Bistrot Hipster garden bistro-bar beneath

trees in Santarosa gardens. (p137)

Flò Summertime terrace bar with dancing, drinks and city views to die for. (p126)

Bar Open: Top Tips

○ Join locals drinking their coffee standing at the cafe's *banco* (bar counter) – it is three to four times cheaper than a coffee ordered sitting at a table.

○ There is one cardinal rule: milky coffee such as cappuccino, *caffe latte* or *latte macchiato* is only ever drunk in the early morning – never, ever, after a meal when the coffee to drink is strictly espresso.

Treasure Hunt

In medieval and Renaissance Florence, goldsmiths, silversmiths and shoemakers were as highly regarded as sculptors and artists. Today, Florentines are equally enamoured of design and artisanship and go out of their way to source quality goods. Most are also happy to pay a considerable amount to fare la bella figura (cut a fine figure).

Fashion

Florentines take great pride in their dress and appearance, which is not surprising given the Italian fashion industry was born here. Guccio Gucci and Salvatore Farragamo got the haute-couture ball rolling in the 1920s, and the first Italian prêt-à-porter show was staged here in 1951.

Via de' Tornabuoni and its surrounding streets are home to upmarket designers from Italy and abroad. Some up-and-coming designers are also here, although most are across the river in the Oltrarno and Santa Croce.

Arts & Crafts

Cheap imported handbags are common, especially in the city's main leather market, Mercato Nuovo (pictured; p47). But for serious shoppers keen to delve into a city synonymous with craftsmanship, there are ample traditional boutiques and *botteghe* (workshops) to visit. Many are in the neighbourhood of Oltrarno, south of the Arno.

Traditional artisan wares produced by hand or on centuries-old machinery include jewellery, leather goods, fabrics and stationery.

Best Fashion

Benheart Leather shoes and jackets by a talented, street-smart Florentine. (p72)

Boutique Nadine Super-chic vintage fashion. (p61)

Bjørk Trendy concept store in the Oltrarno. (p140)

A Piedi Nudi nel Parco High-end, avant-garde designer fashion. (p61)

RARRARORRO/SHUTTERSTOCK ©

Best Accessories

Aprosio & Co Jewellery and accessories crafted from zillions of tiny beads. (p74)

Grevi Romantic millinery boutique. (p74)

Best Food & Drink

La Bottega della Frutta Food shop bursting with boutique produce. (p72)

Obsequium Serious wine shop, with tastings. (p140)

Mercato Centrale Central covered food market in San Lorenzo. (p85)

Best Souvenirs

Officina Profumo-Farmaceutica di

Santa Maria Novella Herbal remedies and beauty products in a pharmacy from 1612. (p73)

Clet Hacked street signs; limited editions of the real thing. (p125)

Best Crafts

Scriptorium Handcrafted leather books, boxes and wax seals in a *palazzo* boutique. (p93)

Worth a Trip: Designer Outlets

Barberino Designer Outlet (☎ 055 84 21 61; www.mcarthurglen.it; Via Meucci, Barberino di Mugello; ⏰ 10am-9pm; 📶) is 40km north of Florence; buses from Piazza della Stazione.

Mall (☎ 055 865 77 75; www.themall.it; Via Europa 8, Leccio Reggello; ⏰ 9.30am-7.30pm Jun-Aug, 10am-7pm Sep-May) is 30km south-east of Florence; buses from SITA bus station between 8.50am and 1pm, returns between 2pm and 6.30pm.

Architecture

A trio of architectural styles are showcased in Florence: Romanesque, Tuscan Gothic and Renaissance. The last originated here – before taking the rest of Italy and Europe by storm – and is the city's emblematic style.

Romanesque

A blow-in from Northern Europe, Romanesque architecture received a unique local twist in Tuscany, where church facades were given alternating stripes of green and white marble. Generally, Romanesque buildings displayed an emphasis on width and the horizontal lines of a building rather than height, and featured church groups with *campaniles* (bell towers) and baptistries that were separate to the church.

Gothic

Tuscans didn't embrace the Gothic as enthusiastically as their northern neighbours; the flying buttresses, grotesque gargoyles and over-the-top decoration were too far from the classical ideal that was bred in the Tuscan bone. There were, of course, exceptions; most notably Siena's *duomo* (cathedral; pictured).

Renaissance

When the dome of Florence's Duomo was completed in 1436, Leon Battista Alberti called it the first great achievement of the 'new' architecture, one that equalled or even surpassed the great buildings of antiquity. The elegance of line, innovation in building method and references to antiquity that characterised Brunelleschi's work were emulated by other Florentine architects, leading to this pared-down, classically inspired style dominating local architecture throughout the 15th and 16th centuries.

RASTOS/SHUTTERSTOCK ©

Best Romanesque

Basilica di San Miniato al Monte An 11th-century church with fine crypt. (p122)

Basilica di Santa Maria Novella Transitional from Romanesque to Gothic. (p64)

Battistero di San Giovanni Octagonal structure with striking green-and-white marble exterior. (p39)

Best Tuscan Gothic

Opera della Metropolitana di Siena Polychrome marble facade (pictured) and black-and-white striped interior. (p156)

Duomo Exquisite facade and elegant *campanile*. (p36)

Museo Civico, Siena Inside the Palazzo Pubblico, whose concave facade complements the convex curve of Piazza del Campo. (p161)

Best Renaissance

Duomo Brunelleschi's dome is considered the finest and most influential achievement of Renaissance architecture. (p36)

Museo degli Innocenti Classically elegant loggia. (p84)

Cappella de' Pazzi, Basilica di Santa Croce Sublimely beautiful exercise in architectural harmony. (p101)

Architecture: Top Tip

Guided walking tours of the city are a great way to learn about and appreciate its architecture. Recommended operators include **ArtViva** (☏055 264 50 33; www.artviva.com; Via de' Sassetti 1) and **Florence Town** (☏055 28 11 03; www.florencetown.com; Piazza della Repubblica 1; ⏱7.30am-8pm summer, 8.30am-6.30pm winter).

Art & Culture

Florence has always embraced art and culture. Few artistic works remain from its days as a Roman colony, but plenty date from the Middle Ages, when the city first hit its artistic stride. Funded by bankers, merchants and guilds, artists adorned the city with frescoes, sculptures and paintings. This continued through the Renaissance, bequeathing Florentines a truly extraordinary artistic heritage.

Medieval Art

The Middle Ages may have been blighted by famines, plagues and wars, but it also saw the rise of civic culture in the Italian city-states, a phenomenon that led to an extraordinary flowering of painting and sculpture. When the Gothic style was imported from Northern Europe, local artists reworked it into a uniquely Tuscan form, creating works that were both sophisticated and elegant and that highlighted attention to detail, a luminous palette and increasingly refined techniques.

Renaissance Art

During the 15th century, painting overtook its fellow disciplines of sculpture and architecture and became the pre-eminent art form for the first time in the history of Western art. Painters experimented with perspective and proportion and took a new interest in realistic portraiture. Supported by wealthy patrons such as the Medici, Florentine painters including Giotto di Bondone, Sandro Botticelli, Tommaso di Simone (Masaccio), Piero della Francesca, Fra' Angelico and Domenico Ghirlandaio were among many artistic innovators.

Best Frescoes

Basilica di Santa Maria Novella Panels by Ghirlandaio and Masaccio's *Trinity*. (p64)

Cappella Brancacci Masaccio's *The Expulsion of Adam and Eve from Paradise* and *The Tribute Money*. (p132)

Palazzo Medici-Riccardi Benozzo Gozzoli's *Journey*

of the Magi in the Cappella dei Magi. (p85)

Museo di San Marco Fra' Angelicos galore, including his *Annunciation* (pictured). (p83)

Museo Civico, Siena Simone Martini's *Maestà* and Ambrogio Lorenzetti's *Allegories of Good and Bad Government*. (p161)

Collegiata, San Gimignano Taddeo di Bartolo's *The Last Judgment* and Domenico Ghirlandaio's *Santa Fina* panels. (p172)

Opera della Metropolitana di Siena Bernardino Pinturicchio's *Life of Pius II* in the Libreria Piccolomini. (p156)

Museo dell'Opera, Siena Duccio di Buoninsegna's *Maestà*. (p158)

Basilica di Santa Croce The Giotto panels in Cappella Bardi and Cappella Peruzzi. (p100)

Best Paintings

Galleria degli Uffizi Paintings by every major Italian Renaissance artist. (p42)

Pinacoteca Nazionale, Siena Gothic masterpieces from the Sienese school. (p163)

Museo Nazionale di San Matteo, Pisa Paintings from the medieval Tuscan school. (p149)

Basilica di San Lorenzo Fra' Filippo Lippi's *Annunciation*. (p82)

Palazzo Pitti Stellar collection of 16th- to 18th-century works in Galleria Palatina. (p116)

Best Sculptures

Museo del Bargello Donatello's *Davids* and early Michelangelos. (p102)

Galleria dell'Accademia Michelangelo's *David* and his *Prigioni* ('Prisoners' or 'Slaves'). (p78)

Museo delle Cappelle Medicee A trio of haunting Michelangelo sculptures. (p82)

Grande Museo del Duomo Ghiberti's *Door of Paradise* panels and Michelangelo's *La Pietà*. (p40)

Duomo & Battistero, Pisa Giovanni and Nicola Pisano's twin set of pulpits. (p145)

Palazzo Vecchio Michelangelo's *Genius of Victory* in the Salone dei Cinquecento. (p52)

Views

CHISLOVAARINA/SHUTTERSTOCK ©

Best Views from Monuments

Campanile & Dome, Duomo Has 360-degree city views. (p39)

Galleria degli Uffizi Snapshots of riverside Florence. (p42)

Palazzo Vecchio Bird's-eye view atop crenellated Torre d'Arnolfo. (p52)

Leaning Tower, Pisa Admire the tower (pictured), Piazza dei Miracoli and the Apuane Alps beyond. (p145)

Torre del Mangia, Siena Vertiginous viewpoint of Campo action. (p163)

Panorama del Facciatone, Siena Quintessential, terracotta-coloured rooftop views. (p159)

Basilica di San Miniato al Monte Admire Florence laid out at your feet. (p122)

Museo degli Innocenti Lounge between chimney pots and sculptures in the museum's rooftop cafe with view extraordinaire. (p84)

Best Views from Public Spaces

Piazzale Michelangelo See Florence unfurled from the city's most spectacular vantage point, preferably at sunset. (p123)

Ponte Vecchio The most romantic sunset view in Florence. (p134)

Best Dining with a View

La Leggenda dei Frati Michelin-starred garden dining with impossibly romantic city panorama. (p124)

Santarosa Bistrot Pretty garden views in a hipster bistro-bar near the river. (p137)

Irene Front-row seats on Piazza della Repubblica. (p55)

La Reggia degli Etruschi, Fiesole Stupendous views over Florence. (p97)

Villa Aurora, Fiesole Fabulous Florentine panorama from a pagoda-covered lunch terrace. (p97)

Best View-Fuelled Drinks

La Terrazza Lounge Bar Chic setting in which to watch the sun set over the Arno. (p57)

La Loggia Sweeping city views up high on Piazzale Michelangelo. (p126)

Showtime

Hanging out on warm summer nights on cafe and bar terraces aside, Florence enjoys a varied nightlife scene thanks in part to its substantial foreign-student population. The city has highly regarded theatres and – from around midnight once aperitivi (pre-dinner drinks) and dinner are done – a fairly low-key but fun dance scene.

T PHOTOGRAPHY/SHUTTERSTOCK ©

Best Dance Clubs

Flò Summer-only venue with themed lounge areas and a dance floor. (p126)

Full Up Eternally popular club with the 20-something crowd, going strong since the 1950s. (p111)

Space Club Dancing, drinking and video-karaoke among a mixed, student-international crowd. (p72)

YAB Over-30s head here on Thursdays, students on other nights. (p61)

Best Live Performance Venues

Il Teatro del Sale Dinner followed by a performance of drama, music or comedy. (p105)

Le Murate Film screenings, book readings, live music and art exhibitions. (p110)

Volume Music, art and DJs in an old hat-making workshop. (p139)

Best Live Music

Dolce Vita Live bands cap off the packed after-dark agenda at this busy Oltrarno lounge bar. (p139)

Lion's Fountain Irish pub with live music. (p111)

Quelo Live bands in a 1950s vintage interior. (p111)

La Cité Vibrant alternative live-music space. (p139)

Best Classical Music

Teatro della Pergola Classical concerts in a beautiful old city theatre. (p139)

Teatro del Maggio Musicale Fiorentino The city's opera house (pictured), host to Florence's annual springtime Maggio Musicale Fiorentino festival. (p72)

Active Florence & Tuscany

Urban and art rich to the core, Florence is hardly a hardcore activity centre: cooking, paddling along the Arno or indulging in a morning jog along its grassy riverbanks, up narrow stone-walled lanes to San Miniato al Monte or in Parco delle Cascine is about as active as most Florentines get.

BALLONI GIOVANNI/SHUTTERSTOCK ©

Best Climbs

Campanile, Duomo Climb 414 steps up Giotto's 85m belltower. (p39)

Cupola, Duomo There are 463 steps winding up the inside edge of Brunelleschi's extraordinary 114m dome. (p37)

Torre d'Arnolfo All 418 steps up the Palazzo Vecchio's 94m tower (pictured). (p52)

Panorama del Facciatone, Siena Just 131 steps to the top of the never-finished New Cathedral. (p159)

Best Guided Tours

ArtViva Urban walks and runs, some themed. (p17)

Florence Town Excellent one-stop shop for a range of city-based tours and activities. (p17)

Palazzo Vecchio Take the 'Secret Passages' or 'Experiencing the Palace First-Hand' tours. (p52)

Giardino Torrigiani Let an Italian aristocrat show you his garden. (p107)

Best Passeggiatas

City Wall, Lucca Along the path atop this Renaissance-era wall. (p153)

Piazza del Campo, Siena Join the throng milling around in Siena's central sloping square. (p161)

Orto e Museo Botanico, Pisa Escape the tourist crowd with a leafy *passeggiata* (evening stroll) in Pisa's peaceful botanical garden. (p150)

Best Bike Rides

Fiesole to Florence A sunset ride guided by FiesoleBike. (p97)

City Wall, Lucca Hire a bike and use pedal power to circle the city. (p153)

Romance

Few cities are as romantic as Florence. Come here to picnic in historic gardens, watch the sun set over the Arno or wander hand-in-hand through ancient cobbled streets. On the practical side, intimate restaurants with dinner tables for two are easy to find, as are luxury and designer hotels.

STELA SUBASHI/SHUTTERSTOCK ©

Best Places to Stay

Ad Astra Contemporary-design guesthouse with romantic views over a historic walled garden. (p177)

Palazzo Vecchietti Hopelessly romantic rooms, some with private terraces. (p177)

Palazzo Magnani Feroni (www.palazzomagnaniferoni.com) Opulent *palazzo*.

Hotel Orto de' Medici Enchanting midranger with intimate garden. (p177)

Best Restaurants

Enoteca Pinchiorri The ultimate seduction: triple Michelin-starred dining. (p109)

La Leggenda dei Frati Garden dining with sweeping Florence panorama. (p124)

Il Santo Bevitore Candlelit tables and Modern Tuscan cuisine. (p133)

Obicà Sofa seating in an elegant, star-topped courtyard. (p57)

Best Picnics

Santarosa Bistrot Grab a picnic to share in this riverside garden with your loved one. (p137)

La Toraia Lounge riverside over burgers from this savvy food truck. (p110)

Best Intimate Strolls

Palazzo Pfanner, Lucca Mooch between lemon trees and Greek-god statues in the intimate garden of a 17th-century palace. (p153)

Villa e Giardino Bardini Historic villa and gardens with ample secret nooks and crannies. (pictured; p122)

City Wall, Lucca Experience the sacrosanct *passeggiata* atop 16th-century city walls. (p153)

Best Sunset Drinks

La Terrazza Lounge Bar Watch the sun set over the Arno over rooftop cocktails. (p57)

La Loggia Sit beneath elegant arches and watch the sun set over the city. (p126)

Under the Radar

PETERVRABEL/SHUTTERSTOCK ©

Since the COVID-19 pandemic emptied Florence of its notoriously overwhelming tourist crowds in early 2020, the Renaissance city has worked hard to reinvent its tourism wheel. The new policy is about enticing enthusiastic visitors away from the tourist-packed spots and encouraging them to explore offbeat, under-the-radar Florence instead.

Best Contemporary Creatives

Betti Soldi (www.bettysoldi.com) Watch for exciting collaborations between the city's leading calligrapher and other artists, designers, florists, jewellers, leather artisans and crafters.

Manufattura Tabacchi (www.manifattura tabacchi.com) A 1930s tobacco factory is now an exciting 'non-museum' tapping into today's dynamic artist, artisan and designer community.

Lady Ripple (www.lady ripple.com) This eco-brand promoting biodiversity, sustainability and bee awareness is a beautiful example of how new renaissance creatives are rethinking art.

Best Hidden Rooftops

Angel Roofbar Admire the city from a bewitching 360-degree perspective at this fashionable roof bar atop Hotel Calimala, Piazza della Repubblica. (www. hotelcalimala.com)

Student Hotel The skyline sky bar for travellers without a sky-high budget. (www. thestudenthotel.com/florence-lavagnini)

Caffè del Verone There is nothing chichi about this down-to-earth rooftop loggia – just good old-fashioned drinks and hopelessly romantic skyline views. (p90)

Best Alternative Sunset Spots

Giardino delle Rose Inhale the scent of 400 rose varieties (late spring is best) and aromatic lemon trees in this 19th-century hillside garden with view (pictured).

Giardino dell'Iris Magical sunset views from this rare iris garden, planted in 1954 as show garden for Florence's International Iris Competition; open for four weeks in late April and May.

Monte Morello Head north out of town and up this mountain to swoon over an insatiable panorama of city of Florence.

For Families

Children are welcomed anywhere, anytime in Florence. Families frequently go out with young children in the evenings, and pasta-rich dining is generally relaxed, straightforward and easy. Some museums run engaging themed tours and workshops, and there are several city parks and riverside paths for kids to run wild post–museum visit.

ALBERTO MASNOVO/SHUTTERSTOCKS ©

Best for Toddlers

Giardino di Boboli Statues, open spaces, hidden paths and a really weird 'face' sculpture. (p119)

Piazza della Repubblica Ride a vintage carousel (pictured). (p54)

Parco delle Cascine Open-air swimming pool and toddler-friendly playgrounds. (p70)

Best for Big Kids

Palazzo Strozzi Art workshops, tours and other artsy activities for families. (p54)

Palazzo Vecchio Climb the Torre d'Arnolfo and tour the palace's secret passages. (p52)

Duomo Climb up Giotto's bell tower or into Brunelleschi's dome. (p36)

Museo Galileo History of science museum; interactive displays. (p54)

Best for Teenagers

Street Levels Gallery Brush up on the local street-art scene. (p68)

FiesoleBike Cycle by sunset ride from Fiesole to Florence. (p97)

Aquaflor Learn about the exotic world of fragrance with a master perfumer. (p112)

Clet Watch Florence's master street-sign hacker at work in his Oltrarno studio. (p125)

Family Travel: Top Tips

o Children with EU passports under 18 receive free entry to many museums.

o Many streets are too crowded and cobbled, and pavements too narrow, to push a stroller along – bring a backpack carrier instead.

Four Perfect Days

Day 1

Journey into the Renaissance with a morning of 15th- and 16th-century art at the **Galleria degli Uffizi** (p42). Break for coffee on a rooftop terrace then clear your head with a stroll in **Piazza della Signoria** (pictured; p53).

Meander south and cross **Ponte Vecchio** (p134), looking for hacked street signs by **Clet** (p125). Explore **Basilica di Santo Spirito** (p132) and magnificent **Cappella Brancacci** (p132). As the sun sinks, hike to **Piazzale Michelangelo** (p123) for swoon-worthy views of the city followed by *aperitivi* at **Le Volpi e l'Uva** (p125).

Stay on the Oltrarno for a sensational dinner at **Essenziale** (p132) or **Burro e Acciughe** (p133), then hit San Frediano for cocktails at **Mad Souls & Spirits** (p137) or **Dolce Vita** (p139).

Day 2

The morning belongs to Piazza del Duomo (pictured): visit the **cathedral** (p36), climb its **campanile** (p39), duck into its **baptistry** (p39) and end high in the frescoed dome of Brunelleschi's **cupola** (p37). Complete the story inside the **Grande Museo del Duomo** (p40).

Lunch at **Irene** (p55) or **Trattoria Le Mossacce** (p55). Window-shop on Via de' Tornabuoni then mooch west, along boutique shopping streets Via della Spada or Via della Vigna Nova, to **Basilica di Santa Maria Novella** (p64). Cross Ponte alla Carraia for a gourmet *aperitivo* at **Il Santino** (p138).

Dine at **Il Santo Bevitore** (p133) then grab a gelato from **Gelateria La Carraia** (p136) to enjoy on a riverside walk. Later, dance to jazz and quaff cocktails beneath the stars at **Santarosa Bistrot** (p137).

Day 3

Begin the day in San Marco with Michelangelo's original *David*, at the **Galleria dell'Accademia** (p78). Continue to the uplifting **Museo di San Marco** (pictured; p83) and end the morning with the emotive **Museo degli Innocenti** (p84).

Grab a quick lunch at **Pugi** (p90). Saunter south to Piazza della Signoria, where the most famous *David* copy guards Palazzo Vecchio. Duck east to **Museo del Bargello** (p102), then back to **Palazzo Vecchio** (p52) to visit the fortress palace and catch sunset views from the top of Torre d'Arnolfo. Savour an *aperitivo* at **Coquinarius** (p59).

Dine at **Il Teatro del Sale** (p105) or **Trattoria Cibrèo** (p108); at the former, enjoy the theatre show. Otherwise, explore Santa Croce by night.

Day 4

Begin with a coffee inside San Lorenzo's buzzing **Mercato Centrale** (pictured; p85) then weave your way south to **Basilica di San Lorenzo** (p82), **Biblioteca Medicea Laurenziana** (p82) and dazzling **Museo delle Cappelle Medicee** (p82). End with a market eatery lunch: at **Da Nerbone** (p87), **Trattoria Mario** (p86) or the **Mercato Centrale** (p85) food hall.

Spend the afternoon exploring the galleries and garden of **Palazzo Pitti** (p116). Pop into nearby **Giardino Bardini** (p118) – a path links it with Pitti's Giardino di Boboli – and end with a drink at **Enoteca Pitti Gola e Cantina** (p139).

Dinner is an upmarket affair at **La Leggenda dei Frati** (p124). Enjoy a cocktail and twinkling views up high at **Flò** (p126).

Need to Know

For detailed information, see Survival Guide (p175)

Currency
euro (€)

Language
Italian

Visas
Not needed for
Schengen countries or
many visitors staying
less than 90 days.

Money
ATMs are widespread.
Credit cards accepted
at most hotels and
many restaurants.

Mobile Phones
Local SIM cards can
be used in European
and Australian phones.
Other phones must be
set to roaming.

Time
One hour ahead of
GMT/UTC. Daylight
saving (clocks are put
forward one hour)
from the last Sunday
in March to the last
Sunday in October.

Tipping
Most visitors leave 10%
to 15% in restaurants
if there's no service
charge.

Daily Budget

Budget: Less than €90

Dorm bed: €18–45

Sandwich: €3–8

Trattoria dinner: €15–25

Midrange: €90–200

Double room in a midrange hotel: €110–200

Restaurant meal: €30–45

Aperitivo: €10

Top End: More than €200

Double room in a four- or five-star hotel: €200 plus

Upmarket restaurant meal: €45–70

Walking tours: €20–50

Useful Websites

Lonely Planet (www.lonelyplanet.com/italy/florence)
Destination information.

The Florentine (www.theflorentine.net) English-language
newspaper.

Girl in Florence (www.girlinflorence.com) Smart drinking
and dining recommendations from American Georgette, at
home in Florence.

Lost in Florence (www.lostinflorence.it) Boutique openings
in the city.

Advance Planning

Three months before Buy tickets for springtime's Maggio
Musicale Fiorentino.

One month before Book tickets online for the Uffizi, Galleria dell'Accademia and Brunelleschi's cupola at the Duomo.

One week before Make table reservations at gastronomic
hot spots Essenziale and La Leggenda dei Frati.

Getting Around

Florence is mostly easily explored on foot, so tourists have little need to use the city's transport. Exceptions are the bus services to Fiesole and Piazzale Michelangelo. Siena and San Gimignano are easily accessed from Florence by bus. Pisa and Lucca are best reached by train. To explore Chianti you need a car.

🚗 Car & Motorcycle

There are strict ZTLs (*Zone a Traffico Limitato;* Limited Traffic Zones) in Florence, Siena, Pisa, Lucca and San Gimignano. If you drive in them you risk a fine of up to €200. Visit www.comune.fi.it for a map of Florence's ZTL.

🚌 Bus

In Florence, buses and electric minibuses – including bus 13 to Piazzale Michelangelo – start/ terminate at the Autolinee Toscane bus stops opposite the south-eastern exit of Stazione di Santa Maria Novella. Tickets cost €1.20 (€2 on board – drivers don't give change!) and are sold at kiosks, tobacconists and at the **Autolinee Toscane ticket & information office** (📞800 424500; www.at-bus. it; 🕐6.45am-8pm) inside the main ticketing hall at Stazione di Santa Maria Novella. A travel pass valid for one/three/seven days is €5/ 12/18. Upon boarding, time stamp your ticket (punch on board) or risk an on-the-spot €50 fine.

🚕 Taxi

Taxis can't be hailed in the street. Ranks are found close to train and bus stations; in Florence call 055 42 42 or 055 43 90.

🚉 Train

The Italian rail network **Trenitalia** (www.trenitalia.com) is modern and efficient. Check its website for routes, timetables and fares.

SOFIE DELAUW/GETTY IMAGES ©

Florence & Tuscany Neighbourhoods

Pisa (p143)
As well as the world-famous Leaning Tower, Romanesque buildings, Gothic churches and Renaissance piazzas abound in this compact, compelling city.

Santa Maria Novella (p63)
Shoppers have long been drawn to this chic corner of the city, lured by the sophisticated boutiques on Via de' Tornabuoni.

Oltrano (p129)
A beguiling labyrinth of cobbled streets and hidden piazzas sheltering traditional *botteghe* (artisans workshops), bohemian wine bars and foodie hotspots.

Boboli & San Miniato al Monte (p115)
A profusion of parks, gardens and panoramic terraces stretching from the Arno to Piazzale Michelangelo.

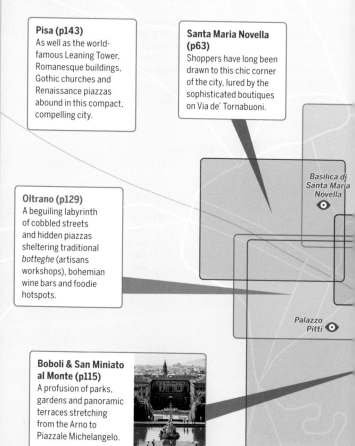

Basilica di Santa Maria Novella ◉

Palazzo Pitti ◉

San Lorenzo & San Marco (p77)
This is Medici territory – home to the family's mansion, parish church and mausoleum.

Duomo to Piazza della Signoria (p35)
The world-famous Galleria degli Uffizi is one of many marvellous museums found in the city's medieval heart.

Galleria dell'Accademia ◉

◉ Duomo

◉ Museo del Bargello

Galleria degli Uffizi ◉

◉ Basilica di Santa Croce

Santa Croce (p99)
The advent of ultrafashionable eateries, bars and clubs has reinvented this ancient residential area.

Siena (p155)
Siena's medieval historic centre is a World Heritage site, with a stunning cathedral and glorious Gothic architecture and art.

Explore
Florence & Tuscany

Worth a Trip 👀

Florence's Walking Tours 🥾

Explore ◈

Duomo to Piazza della Signoria

Hub of the Renaissance and cosmopolitan heart of modern Florence, the enchanting maze of narrow streets between the Duomo and Piazza della Signoria packs one almighty historic and cultural punch. A 'hood harking back to Dante, the Romans and beyond, this is where the city's blockbuster sights – and tourists – mingle with elegant cafes, chic boutiques and the city's swishest shopping strip.

The Short List

○ **Cupola del Brunelleschi (p37)** *Scaling 400-plus steep spiralling steps to explore inside the cathedral's iconic, red-tiled dome.*

○ **Museo dell'Opera del Duomo (p40)** *Getting lost in the compelling back story behind Florence's cathedral and its Renaissance masterpiece of a dome.*

○ **Uffizi (p42)** *Gorging on the world's best Italian Renaissance art.*

○ **Corridoio Vasariano (p52)** *Following in Medici footsteps along this enigmatic, dazzlingly reworked passageway across the Arno.*

Getting There

🚶 From Piazza della Stazione walk southeast along Via de' Panzani and Via de' Cerretani to the Duomo. From here, Piazza della Signoria and the Uffizi are a short walk south down Via dei Calzaluoli.

Duomo to Piazza del Signoria Map on p50

Top Experience 📷

Gaze at the Duomo

Properly titled *Cattedrale di Santa Maria del Fiore (Cathedral of St Mary of the Flower)*, but known as the Duomo (cathedral), this is Florence's iconic landmark. Designed by Sienese architect Arnolfo di Cambio, construction began in 1296 and took almost 150 years. The result – with Brunelleschi's distinctive red-tiled cupola, graceful campanile (bell tower) and pink, white and green marble facade – is breathtaking.

◎ MAP P50, E1

☎ 055 230 28 85

www.museumflorence.com

Piazza del Duomo

admission free

🕙 10am-5pm Mon-Wed & Fri, to 4.30pm Thu & Sat, 1.30-4.45pm Sun

Facade

The neo-Gothic facade was designed in the 19th century by architect Emilio de Fabris to replace the uncompleted original. The oldest and most clearly Gothic part of the structure is its south flank, pierced by the **Porta dei Canonici** (Canons' Door), a mid-14th-century High Gothic creation (you enter here to climb to the dome).

Cupola

When Michelangelo went to work on St Peter's in Rome, he reportedly said, 'I go to build a greater dome, but not a fairer one', referring to the huge but graceful terracotta-brick **dome** (Brunelleschi's Dome; adult/reduced incl baptistry, campanile, crypt & museum €18/3; ⏱8.30am-7pm Mon-Fri, to 5pm Sat, 1-4pm Sun) atop Florence's *duomo*. It was constructed between 1420 and 1436 to a design by Filippo Brunelleschi and is a highlight of any visit to Florence. Its sheer scale alone is breathtaking: 45m wide and 90m high (116m with the crowning lantern).

Interior

After taking in the incredibly richly adorned facade as best as one can, the spartan nature of the *duomo*'s vast interior – 155m long and 90m wide – comes as something of a visual relief. Most of its artistic treasures have been removed and those that remain are unexpectedly secular, reflecting the fact that the *duomo* was built with public funds as a *chiesa di stato* (state church).

Down the left aisle two immense frescoes of equestrian statues portray two *condottieri* (mercenaries) – on the left Niccolò da Tolentino by Andrea del Castagno (1456), and on the right Sir John Hawkwood (who fought in the service of Florence in the 14th century) by Paolo Uccello (1436). In the same aisle, *La Commedia illumina Firenze* (1465) by Domenico di Michelino depicts poet Dante Alighieri surrounded by the three afterlife worlds he describes in the *Divine*

★ Top Tips

○ Dress code is strict: no shorts, miniskirts or sleeveless tops.

○ One ticket covers all the sights and is valid for 48 hours (one visit per sight); purchase at www.ilgrandemuseodelduomo.it or at the **ticket office** (Piazza San Giovanni 7; ⏱8.15am-6.45pm), opposite the baptistry entrance.

○ Reservations are obligatory for the Duomo's cupola; book a time slot when buying your ticket online or at a self-service Ticketpoint machine inside the Piazza di San Giovanni ticket office.

✗ Take a Break

Post-Duomo, savour modern Tuscan cuisine at contemporary bistro Irene (p55).

Wine bar Coquinarius (p59) is perfect for a dusk-time *aperitivo* with snacks.

Comedy: purgatory is behind him, his right hand points towards hell, and the city of Florence is paradise.

Clock

Upon entering the *duomo*, look up to see its clock with fantastic, 4.6m-wide frescoed face resembling a flower. One of Europe's first monumental – and unconventional – clocks, it notably turns in an anticlockwise direction, counts in 24 hours starting at the bottom and begins the first hour of the day at sunset (rather than midnight).

The clock was painted by eclectic Florentine painter Paolo Uccello (1397–1495) between 1440 and 1443. To this day, it is lovingly tended to by two caretakers who, every few days, enter the tiny door on ground level below the clock, climb the steep narrow staircase hidden between the *duomo's* thick interior and exterior walls, and adjust the clock mechanism to take into account the changing hour of sunset.

In Renaissance Florence, the cathedral bells rang three times a day: when the *duomo's* single petal-shaped clock hand pointed to 23 (to prayer), 24 (sunset, when the work day officially ended and the city gates closed for the day) and at 1 (the start of a new 'day'). The Florentine expression *Alle porte con i sassi* (literally 'to be at the gate with stones'), meaning one is up to their ears in it, or only just keeping their head above water, refers to Florentines who, in the Middle Ages, rushing to return to their homes outside the walled city, would throw stones at the city gates to warn the gatekeeper of their pending arrival.

Campanile

Mass Sacristy

Between the left (north) arm of the transept and the apse is the **Sagrestia delle Messe** (Mass Sacristy), accessible only by guided tour. All four walls are panelled in a marvel of inlaid wood carved by Benedetto and Giuliano da Maiano between 1436 and 1468. The fine bronze doors were executed by Luca della Robbia – his only known work in the material. Above the doorway is his glazed terracotta *Resurrezione* (Resurrection).

Crypt of Santa Reparata

Excavated remains of the very first church that stood on this site, the 5th-century Chiesa di Santa Reparata, can be admired in the Duomo's **Cripta Santa Reparata** (adult/reduced incl cupola, baptistry, campanile & museum €18/3; ☻10am-5pm Mon-Wed & Fri, to 4.30pm Thu & Sat) – access it from the staircase, not far from the main entrance, in the south aisle. Down below, secreted among the ancient stones, are the cathedral gift shop, remains of Roman dwellings, marble floor mosaics (for early Christians the peacock was a symbol of eternal life) and the tomb of 15th-century architect Filippo Brunelleschi.

Campanile

Set next to the *duomo* is its slender **campanile** (Bell Tower; adult/reduced incl baptistry, cupola, crypt & museum €18/3; ☻8.15am-7pm), a striking work of Florentine Gothic architecture designed by Giotto, the artistic genius often described as the founding artist of the Renaissance. The steep 414-step climb up the square, 85m-tall tower offers the reward of a view that is nearly as impressive as that from the dome.

The first tier of bas-reliefs around the base of its elaborate Gothic facade are copies of those carved by Pisano depicting the creation of humanity and the *attività umane* (arts and industries). Those on the second tier depict the planets, the cardinal virtues, the arts and the seven sacraments. The sculpted prophets and sibyls in the upper-storey niches are copies of works by Donatello and others.

Baptistry

Across from the *duomo's* main entrance is the 11th-century **Battistero di San Giovanni** (Baptistry; adult/reduced incl campanile, cupola, crypt & museum €18/3; ☻8.15-10.15am & 11.15am-7.30pm Mon-Fri, 8.15am-6.30pm Sat, 8.15am-1.30pm Sun), an octagonal, striped structure of white-and-green marble. Dante is among the famous people to have been dunked in its baptismal font – still used every third Sunday of the month to baptise babies born within the surrounding San Lorenzo parish.

The Romanesque structure is most celebrated, however, for its three sets of doors illustrating the story of humanity and the Redemption. The gilded bronze doors by Lorenzo Ghiberti at the eastern entrance, the *Porta del Paradiso* (Gate of Paradise), are copies –

the originals are in the Museo dell'Opera del Duomo. Andrea Pisano executed the southern doors (1330), illustrating the life of St John the Baptist, and Lorenzo Ghiberti won a public competition in 1401 to design the northern doors, likewise replaced by copies today.

The baptistry's interior gleams with Byzantine-style mosaics. Covering the dome in five horizontal tiers, they include scenes from the lives of St John the Baptist, Christ and Joseph on one side, and a representation of the Last Judgement on the other. A choir of angels surveys proceedings from the innermost tier.

Buy tickets online or at the Piazza di San Giovanni ticket office (p37).

Grande Museo del Duomo

This awe-inspiring **museum** (Cathedral Museum; Piazza del Duomo 9; adult/reduced incl cathedral bell tower, cupola, baptistry & crypt €15/3; ⏱9am-7pm) tells the magnificent story of how the Duomo and its cupola was built through art and short films.

The museum's spectacular main hall, **Sala del Paradiso**, is dominated by a life-size reconstruction of the original facade of the Duomo, decorated with some forty 14th- and early-15th-century statues carved for the facade by 14th-century masters. Building work began in 1296 but it was never finished and in 1587 the facade was eventually dismantled. This is also where you will find Ghiberti's original 15th-century masterpiece, *Porta del Paradiso* (1425–52; *Doors of Paradise*) – gloriously golden, 16m-tall gilded bronze doors

designed for the eastern entrance to the Baptistry – as well as those he sculpted for the northern entrance (1403–24).

Continuing up to the 1st floor, **Rooms 14 and 15** explain in detail just how Brunelleschi constructed the ground-breaking cathedral dome. Look at 15th-century tools, pulleys, tackles and hoisting wagons used to build the cupola, watch a film and admire Brunelleschi's funeral mask (1446).

Scaling Brunelleschi's Dome

One of the finest masterpieces of the Renaissance, the cupola crowning the Duomo is a feat of engineering and one that cannot be fully appreciated without climbing its 463 interior stone steps. Taking his inspiration from Rome's Pantheon, Filippo Brunelleschi (1377–1446) – architect, mathematician, engineer and sculptor – spent an incredible 42 years working on the dome. Starting work in 1419, his mathematical brain and talent for devising innovative engineering solutions enabled him to do what many Florentines had thought impossible: deliver the largest dome to be built in Italy since antiquity.

Brunelleschi arrived at an innovative engineering solution of a distinctive octagonal shape of inner and outer concentric domes resting on the drum of the cathedral rather than the roof itself, allowing artisans to build from the ground up without needing a wooden support frame. Over four million bricks were used in the construction, all of them laid in consecutive rings in horizontal courses using a vertical herring-bone pattern.

The climb up the spiral staircase is relatively steep, and should not be attempted if you are claustrophobic. Make sure to pause when you reach the balustrade at the base of the dome, which gives an aerial view of the octagonal *coro* (choir) of the cathedral below and the seven round stained-glass windows (by Donatello, Andrea del Castagno, Paolo Uccello and Lorenzo Ghiberti) that pierce the octagonal drum.

Look up and you'll see the flamboyant late-16th-century frescoes by Giorgio Vasari and Federico Zuccari, depicting the *Giudizio Universale* (Last Judgement; 1572–79) and decorating the 4500-sq-m surface of the cupola's inner dome is one of the world's largest paintings. Look for a spent Mother Nature with wrinkled breasts and the four seasons asleep at her feet. Less savoury are the poor souls in hell being sodomised with a pitchfork.

As you climb, snapshots of Florence can be spied through small windows. The final leg – a straight, somewhat hazardous flight up the curve of the inner dome – rewards with an unforgettable 360-degree panorama of one of Europe's most beautiful cities.

Tribuna di Michelangelo

Michelangelo's achingly beautiful *Pietà*, sculpted when he was almost 80 and intended for his own tomb, is displayed here. Dissatisfied with both the quality of the marble and of his own work, Michelangelo broke up the unfinished sculpture, destroying the arm and left leg of the figure of Christ.

Sala del Tresoro

Precious treasures from the Duomo buildings are stashed in the 1st-floor Treasury: don't miss the dazzling altar and monumental cross, crafted from 250kg of pure silver. The twin set was commissioned by Florence's wealthy cloth merchants' guild and executed in 1367 by silversmiths and artists spanning several generations.

Rooftop Terrace

This neighbourhood has ample high points from which to admire Florence's Renaissance splendour: one less known, not to be missed for its larger-than-life cupola views, is the Grande Museo del Duomo's hidden rooftop terrace.

Top Experience 📷

Discover Renaissance Art at the Galleria degli Uffizi

Home to the world's greatest collection of Italian Renaissance art, Florence's premier gallery occupies the vast U-shaped Palazzo degli Uffizi. As part of the ongoing Nuovi Uffizi project, the permanent collection has grown from 45 to 101 revamped rooms; but work remains on temporary-exhibition areas. Expect some halls to be closed, the contents of others changed.

◉ MAP P50, E6

Uffizi Gallery

☎ 055 29 48 83

www.uffizi.it

Piazzale degli Uffizi 6

adult/reduced Mar-Oct €20/2, Nov-Feb €12/2

🕐 8.15am-6.50pm Tue-Sun

Tuscan 13th-Century Art

Arriving in the **Primo Corridoio** (First Corridor) on the 2nd floor, the first room to the left of the staircase (Room 2) is designed like a medieval chapel to reflect its fabulous contents: three large altarpieces from Florentine churches by Tuscan masters Duccio di Buoninsegna, Cimabue and Giotto. They show the transition from Gothic to nascent Renaissance style.

Sienese 14th-Century Art

The highlight in Room 3 is Simone Martini's shimmering *Annunciazione* (1333), painted with Lippo Memmi and setting the Madonna in a sea of gold. Also of note is *Madonna con il bambino in trono e angeli* (Madonna with Child and Saints; 1340) by Pietro Lorenzetti, which demonstrates a realism similar to Giotto's; unfortunately, both Pietro and his artistic brother Ambrogio died of the plague in Siena in 1348.

Renaissance Pioneers

Perspective was a hallmark of the early-15th-century Florentine school (Room 8) that launched the Renaissance. One panel from Paolo Uccello's striking *Battle of San Romano* (1436–40), which celebrates Florence's victory over Siena in 1432, shows the artist's efforts to create perspective with amusing effect as he directs the lances, horses and soldiers to a central disappearing point. In the same room, don't miss the exquisite *Madonna con bambino e due angeli* (Madonna and Child with Two Angels; 1460–65) by Fra' Filippo Lippi, a Carmelite monk who had an unfortunate soft spot for earthly pleasures and scandalously married a nun from Prato. This work clearly influenced his pupil, Sandro Botticelli.

Duke & Duchess of Urbino

In the same room (Room 8), revel in the realism of Piero della Francesca's 1465 warts-and-all portraits of the Duke and Duchess of Urbino.

★ Top Tips

o Cut out the queue: prebook tickets online (reservation €4) and collect on arrival.

o Check the latest new rooms (and those temporarily closed during expansion works) in the 'News' section of www.uffizi.org.

o Dress light: leave bags in the ground-floor wardrobe by the main entrance, but you are obliged to carry your coat around with you.

o Allow time to linger in the 2nd-floor Secondo Corridoio (Second Corridor) linking the Primo (First) and Terzo (Third) corridors – views of the Arno and Florentine hills beyond are intoxicating.

✗ Take a Break

Head to the Uffizi's rooftop cafe for coffee, fresh air and fabulous views.

Lunch on gourmet *panini*, wine and Tuscan chocolate at 'Ino (p56).

The crooked-nosed duke lost his right eye in a jousting accident, hence the focus on his left side only, while the duchess is deathly stone-white to convey the fact that the portrait was painted posthumously.

Botticelli

The spectacular **Sala del Botticelli**, numbered 10 to 14 but really two light and graceful rooms, is always packed. Of the many Botticelli works displayed in the Uffizi, his iconic *La nascita di Venere* (The Birth of Venus; c 1485), *Primavera* (Spring; c 1482) and *Madonna del Magnificat* (Madonna of the Magnificat; 1483) are the best-known by the Renaissance master known for his ethereal figures. Take time to study the lesser-known *Annunciazione* (Annunciation), a 6m-wide fresco painted by Botticelli in 1481 for the San Martino hospital in Florence.

The Tribune

The Medici clan stashed away their most precious art in this octagonal-shaped treasure trove (Room 18), created by Francesco I between 1581 and 1586. Designed to amaze, it features a small collection of classical statues and paintings on its upholstered silk walls and 6000 crimson-varnished mother-of-pearl shells encrusting the domed ceiling.

Leonardo da Vinci

Three early Florentine works by Leonardo da Vinci dominate Room 35. His *Annunciazione* (Annunciation; 1472) was deliberately painted to be admired not face on, but rather from the lower right-hand side of the painting. *Adoration of the Magi* (1481–82), originally commissioned for the altar of the monastery of San Donato a Scopeto near Florence and never finished, is typical of Florentine figurative painting in the 15th century.

Michelangelo

Michelangelo's dazzling *Doni Tondo*, a depiction of the Holy Family, hangs in Room 41. The composition is unusual and the colours as vibrant as when they were first applied in 1504–06. It was painted for wealthy Florentine merchant Agnolo Doni (who hung it above his bed) and bought by the Medici for Palazzo Pitti in 1594.

Ceiling fresco, Primo Corridoio (p43)

ALZADA STUDIOS/SHUTTERSTOCK ©

The other High Renaissance masterpiece in this room is Raphael's *Madonna col Bambino e San Giovanni* (Madonna with Child and St John; 1505–06), otherwise known as Madonna of the Goldfinch after the red-feathered goldfinch cradled in the chubby hands of a baby John the Baptist. Raphael painted it during his four-year sojourn in Florence and it has been in the Uffizi since 1704.

Contini Bonacossi Collection

Downstairs in the 1st-floor galleries, the star turn of the Donazione Contini Bonacossi (Rooms 46 to 55) is Gian Lorenzo Bernini's voluptuous marble sculpture (1613–17) of the martyred San Lorenzo writhing above flames as he burns alive on a gridiron. It is one of 144 pieces in the private collection of paintings, sculptures, exquisite maiolica ceramics and works by Veronese, Goya and Tintoretto, all left to the state by art collector Contini Bonacossi upon his death in 1955.

Medici Portraits

Room 65 showcases Agnolo Bronzino (1503–72), official portrait artist at the court of Cosimo I. His 1545 portraits of the Grand Duchess Eleonora of Toledo and her son Giovanni together, and the 18-month-old Giovanni alone holding a goldfinch – symbolising his calling into the church – are masterpieces of 16th-century European portraiture.

Palazzo degli Uffizi

Cosimo I de' Medici commissioned Vasari to build the huge U-shaped Palazzo degli Uffizi in 1560 as a government office building (*uffizi* means 'offices'). Following Vasari's death in 1564, architects Alfonso Parigi and Bernado Buontalenti took over, with Buontalenti modifying the upper floor to house the artworks keenly collected by Cosimo I's son, Francesco I. In 1580 the building was complete. When the last Medici died in 1743, the family's enormous private art collection was bequeathed to Florence on the strict proviso that it never leave the city.

Caravaggio

The dramatic, dark blood-red colouring the walls in eight rooms dedicated to the 17th century shows off works by Caravaggio to menacing perfection. The *Head of Medusa* (1598–99), commissioned for a ceremonial shield, is supposedly a self-portrait of the young artist who was deemed vulgar at the time for his direct interpretation of reality and later died at the age of 39. The biblical drama of an angel steadying the hand of Abraham as he holds a knife to his son Isaac's throat in Caravaggio's *Sacrifice of Isaac* (1601–02) is glorious in its intensity.

Walking Tour 🚶

Heart of the City

Every visitor to Florence spends time navigating the cobbled medieval lanes that run between Via de' Tornabuoni and Via del Proconsolo but few explore them thoroughly, instead focusing on the major monuments and spaces. This walk will introduce you to some less visited sights and laneways.

Start Piazza della Repubblica

Finish La Terrazza Lounge Bar

Length 2km; two hours

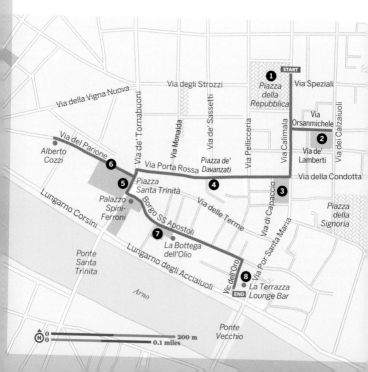

❶ Piazza della Repubblica

Start with a coffee at one of the historic cafes on this handsome 19th-century square (p54). Its construction entailed the demolition of a Jewish ghetto and produce market, and the relocation of nearly 6000 residents.

❷ Chiesa e Museo di Orsanmichele

Follow Via Calimala and Via Orsanmichele to reach this unique church (p52), created in the 14th century when the arcades of a century-old grain market were walled in and two storeys added.

❸ Mercato Nuovo

Back on Via Calimala, walk south to the 16th-century **Mercato Nuovo** (New Market), a covered marketplace awash with stalls selling tourist kitsch and cheap leather goods (definitely *not* made in Tuscany). Look for *Il Porcellino* (The Piglet), a bronze statue of a boar – rub its snout to ensure your return to Florence!

❹ Palazzo Davanzati

On Via Porta Rossa is this 14th-century warehouse residence (p52) with its studded doors and central loggia. A few doors down, next to the Slowly bar, peep through the sturdy iron gate and up to admire ancient brick vaults.

❺ Basilica di Santa Trìnita

Continue to Via de' Tornabuoni, the city's most famous shopping strip. Cross Piazza Santa Trìnita and duck into this church (p69) to admire its frescoed chapels.

❻ Via del Parione

Wander down this narrow street filled with old mansions (now apartments) and artisan workshops. Pop into paper marbler Alberto Cozzi at No 35r to watch local artisans at work.

❼ Chiesa di Santissimi Apostoli

Backtrack to Via de' Tornabuoni and turn right, past 13th-century **Palazzo Spini-Feroni**, home of Salvatore Ferragamo's flagship store, to Borgo Santissimi Apostoli. A short way ahead on Piazza del Limbo is the Romanesque **Chiesa dei Santissimi Apostoli** in a sunken square once used as a cemetery for unbaptised babies.

❽ Hotel Continentale

After browsing for Tuscan olive oil in specialist boutique **La Bottega dell'Olio** at No 4r on the same square, walk east and turn right into Vicolo dell' Oro. The sleek rooftop terrace La Terrazza Lounge Bar (p57) inside Hotel Continentale is the perfect spot for a sundowner with a Ponte Vecchio view.

Walking Tour 🚶

Renaissance Florence

This greatest-hits tour crams a huge amount of culture into a very tight timeline – you'll need to proceed at a cracking pace to see everything in four hours. Alternatively – and preferably – divide it over two days to ensure that you do all of the sights justice.

Start Museo delle Cappelle Medicee

Finish Basilica di Santa Croce

Length 3.2km; minimum four hours

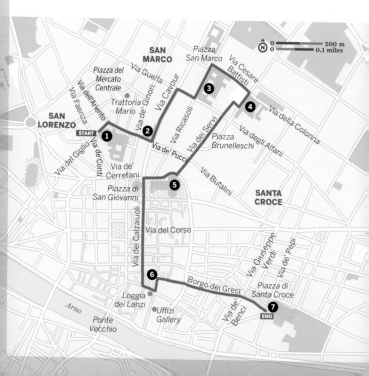

❶ Museo delle Cappelle Medicee

Start in the territory of Renaissance powerbrokers and art patrons, the Medici, who commissioned a number of self-aggrandising monuments in San Lorenzo. The greatest is this mausoleum (p82), partly designed by Michelangelo and containing some of his finest sculptures.

❷ Palazzo Medici-Riccardi

Cross Piazza San Lorenzo to reach this Medici palace (p85), commissioned by Cosimo the Elder and designed by Michelozzo. Admire its facade then head inside to see Benozzo Gozzoli's vivid frescoes in the Cappella dei Magi. Lunch at Trattoria Mario (p86); arrive by noon to snag a table.

❸ Galleria dell'Accademia

Ogle the work of art most synonymous with the Renaissance – Michelangelo's statue of *David* in this art gallery (p78). A powerful evocation of the humanist principles that underpinned this period, it easily lives up to its huge reputation.

❹ Museo degli Innocenti

Make your way to the Brunelleschi-designed loggia of this 15th-century foundling hospital and Europe's first orphanage – today a cutting-edge museum (p84) – which architectural historians credit as one of the great triumphs of Renaissance architecture.

❺ Duomo

Head to the Duomo (p36) and, assuming you have booked your timed slot in advance, climb to the top of its red-tiled dome, another Brunelleschi masterpiece. The 360-degree city panorama is breathtaking.

❻ Piazza della Signoria

Head south down Via del Proconsolo then west to wander through the city's most spectacular piazza (p53), admiring the open-air sculptures under the **Loggia dei Lanzi** and noting the location of the Uffizi – repository of the world's pre-eminent collection of Renaissance art – for future visits.

❼ Basilica di Santa Croce

Trail pedestrianised Borgo dei Greci to reach this huge Franciscan basilica (p100) where Renaissance luminaries including Michelangelo, Machiavelli, Galileo and Ghiberti are buried. Ogle Giotto frescoes in its Cappella Bardi and admire Brunelleschi's exquisite Cappella de' Pazzi.

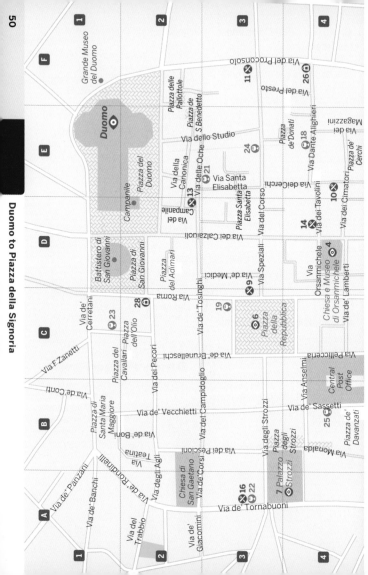

Grande Museo del Duomo

Duomo

Campanile

Piazza del Duomo

Piazza delle Pallottole

Piazza de S Benedetto

Via dello Studio

Via della Canonica

Via delle Oche 21

13

Via del Campanile

Via Santa Elisabetta

Piazza Santa Elisabetta

Via del Corso

Via de' Calzaiuoli

Battistero di San Giovanni

Piazza di San Giovanni

Piazza del Adimari

Via de' Speziali

Via de' Medici

9

Via de' Tosinghi

Via Roma

19

Piazza della Repubblica

6

Via de' Brunelleschi

Via de' Cerretani

23

Piazza del Cavallari

Piazza dell'Olio

28

Via de' Pecori

Via F Zanetti

Via de' Conti

Piazza di Santa Maria Maggiore

Via de' Boni

Via Teatina

Via del Campidoglio

Via de' Vecchietti

Chiesa di San Gaetano

Via de' Corsi

16

22

Palazzo Strozzi

7

Via de' Tornabuoni

Via del Trebbio

Via de' Giacomini

Via de' Banchi

Via de' Panzani

Via de' Rondinelli

Via degli Agli

Via del Pescioni

Piazza degli Strozzi

Via degli Strozzi

Via Anselmi

Via Pellicceria

Via de' Sassetti

Central Post Office

25

Via Monalda

Piazza de' Davanzati

11

26

Via del Procosolo

Via del Presto

Via dei Magazzini

Piazza de Donati

18

Via Dante Alighieri

24

Via del Corso

Via dei Cerchi

Piazza de' Cerchi

10

Via dei Cimatori

Via dei Tavolini

14

Chiesa e Museo di Orsanmichele

Via Orsanmichele

4

Via de' Lamberti

F

E

D

C

B

A

1

2

3

4

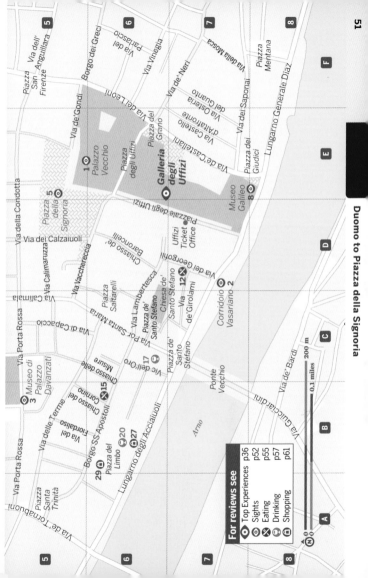

Duomo to Piazza della Signoria

Piazza dell' San-Anguillara 5

Via dell' Anguillara

Piazza San-Anguillara 5

Borgo dei Greci

Via del Palagio 6

Via Vinegia

Piazza Firenze

Via de' Gondi

Via de' Neri

Via della Mosca 7

Piazza del Grano

Via Castello d'Altafronte

Via Osteria del Guanto

Via della Saponai

Piazza Mentana

Palazzo Vecchio 1

Piazza degli Uffizi

Galleria degli Uffizi

Via de' Castellani

Piazza dei Giudici

Lungarno Generale Diaz 8

Via della Condotta

Piazza della Signoria 5

Museo Galileo 8

Via dei Calzaiuoli

Via dei Leoni

Piazzale degli Uffizi

Via Calimaruzza

Chiasso de' Baroncelli

Uffizi Ticket Office

Via dei Georgofili

Corridoio Vasariano 2

Via Calimala

Via Vacchereccia

Piazza Saltarelli

Via de' Girolami

Via Lambertesca

Chiesa di Santo Stefano 12

Via Por Santa Maria

Piazza de' Santo Stefano

Via de' Bardi

Via di Capaccio

Vic dell'Oro 17

Piazza de' Santo Stefano

Via Guicciardini

Museo di Palazzo Davanzati 3

Chiasso delle Misure

Chiasso del Cornino 15

Ponte Vecchio

Via Porta Rossa

Via delle Terme

Via del Fiordaliso

Borgo SS Apostoli

Arno

Via Porta Rossa

Piazza Santa Trinità

Via del Limbo 29

20 27

Lungarno degli Acciaiuoli

Via de' Tornabuoni

200 m

0.1 miles

For reviews see	
Top Experiences	p36
Sights	p52
Eating	p55
Drinking	p57
Shopping	p61

Sights

Palazzo Vecchio   MUSEUM

1 📍 MAP P50, E5

This fortress palace, with its crenellations and 94m-high tower, was designed by Arnolfo di Cambio between 1298 and 1314 for the *signoria* (city government). Today it is home to the mayor's office and the municipal council. From the top of the **Torre d'Arnolfo** (tower), you can revel in unforgettable views. Inside, Michelangelo's *Genio della Vittoria* (Spirit of Victory) sculpture graces the Salone dei Cinquecento, a magnificent painted hall created for the city's 15th-century ruling Consiglio dei Cinquecento (Council of 500). (📞055 276 85 58; www.musefirenze.it; Piazza della Signoria; adult/reduced museum €12.50/10, tower €12.50/10, museum & tower €17.50/15, museum & archaeological tour €16/13.50, combination ticket €19.50/17.50; ⏰museum 9am-11pm Fri-Wed, to 2pm Thu Apr-Sep, 9am-7pm Fri-Wed, to 2pm Thu Oct-Mar, tower 9am-9pm Fri-Wed, to 2pm Thu Apr-Sep, 10am-5pm Fri-Wed, to 2pm Thu Oct-Mar)

Corridoio Vasariano   BRIDGE

2 📍 MAP P50, D7

This 1km-long covered passageway, expected to be reopened in 2022 following restoration work, connects Palazzo Vecchio with the Uffizi (p42) and Palazzo Pitti (p16). Vasari designed it in 1565 to allow the Medici to wander between their palaces in privacy and comfort. When the €10-million renovation is complete, visitors will follow in Medici footsteps past a line-up of antique statues, 16th-century frescoes once adorning the corridor's external walls, and memorials to Florence bombings in 1944 and 1993. Guided visits by Firenze Musei (p179) will be by reservation only. (Vasari Corridor; guided visit by reservation Mar-Oct €45, Nov-Feb €20)

Museo di Palazzo Davanzati   MUSEUM

3 📍 MAP P50, B5

Home to the wealthy Davanzati merchant family from 1578, this 14th-century *palazzo* (mansion) with a wonderful central loggia gives you a view into precisely how Florentine nobles lived in the 16th century. Spot the carved faces of the original owners on the pillars in the inner courtyard, and don't miss the 1st-floor **Sala Madornale** (Reception Room) with its painted wooden ceiling, exotic **Sala dei Pappagalli** (Parrot Room) and **Camera dei Pavoni** (Peacock Bedroom). (📞055 064 94 60; www.bargellomusei.beniculturali.it; Via Porta Rossa 13; adult/reduced €6/3; ⏰8.15am-2pm Mon-Fri, 1.15-7pm Sat & Sun)

Chiesa e Museo di Orsanmichele   CHURCH

4 📍 MAP P50, D4

This unusual and inspirational church, with a Gothic tabernacle by Andrea Orcagna, was created when the arcades of an old grain market (1290) were walled in and two storeys added during the 14th century. Its exterior is decorated with niches and tabernacles bearing statues representing the patron saints of Florence's many guilds, commissioned in the 15th and 16th centuries after the *signoria* (city government) ordered the guilds to finance the church's decoration. (www.bargello musei.beniculturali.it; Via dell'Arte della Lana; admission free; ⏱church 10am-4.50pm daily, closed Mon Aug, museum 10am-4.50pm Mon, 10am-12.30pm Sat)

Piazza della Signoria   PIAZZA

5 ◎ MAP P50, E5

The hub of local life since the 13th century, Florentines flock here to meet friends and chat over early-evening *aperitivi* at historic cafes. Presiding over everything is Palazzo Vecchio, Florence's city hall, and the 14th-century **Loggia dei Lanzi** (admission free), an open-air gallery showcasing Renaissance sculptures, including Giambologna's *Rape of the Sabine Women* (c 1583), Benvenuto Cellini's bronze *Perseus* (1554) and Agnolo Gaddi's *Seven Virtues* (1384–89). Mythological figures frolic in the recently restored **Neptune Fountain**, commissioned in 1559.

Chiesa e Museo di Orsanmichele

Palazzo Vecchio Tours

To get the most out of one of Florence's most dynamic, well-thought-out museums, join one of its excellent guided tours or hands-on workshops that take you into parts of Palazzo Vecchio (p52) that are otherwise inaccessible. Many are in English; you need a valid museum ticket in addition to the guided-tour ticket. Reserve in advance by telephone, email info@muse. comune.fi.it or book at the **Muse Firenze** (☏055 276 82 24; www.musefirenze.it; � reservations 9.30am-1pm & 2.30-5pm Mon-Sat, 9.30am-12.30pm Sun) ticket desk inside Palazzo Vecchio.

Piazza della Repubblica   PIAZZA

6 ◉ MAP P50, C3

The site of a Roman forum and heart of medieval Florence, this busy civic space was created in the 1880s as part of a controversial plan of 'civic improvements' involving the demolition of the old market, Jewish ghetto and slums, and the relocation of nearly 6000 residents. Vasari's lovely Loggia del Pesce (Fish Market) was saved and re-erected on Via Pietrapiana.

Palazzo Strozzi   GALLERY

7 ◉ MAP P50, A4

This 15th-century Renaissance mansion was built for wealthy merchant Filippo Strozzi, one of the Medicis' major political and commercial rivals. Today it hosts exciting art exhibitions spanning all periods and genres – its contemporary art events are particularly sensational. There's always a buzz about the place, with fashionable Florentines milling around the palace's elegant interior courtyard and lingering over drinks at **Strozzi Caffè** (☏055 28 82 36; ☻8am-1am Thu-Sat, to 9.30pm Sun-Wed; ☏); during major exhibitions, grab a coffee to take away from here to enjoy while waiting in line.

Art workshops, tours and other activities aimed squarely at families make the gallery a firm favourite with everyone. If you plan to visit the Museo dell'Opera del Duomo (p40) the same day, buy a combination ticket (adult/reduced €16/6). (☏055 264 51 55; www.palazzostrozzi.org; Piazza degli Strozzi; exhibition adult/reduced €12/4; ☻10am-8pm Fri-Wed, to 11pm Thu; ✚)

Museo Galileo   MUSEUM

8 ◉ MAP P50, E8

On the Arno river next to the Uffizi in 12th-century Palazzo Castellani – look for the sundial telling the time on the pavement outside – is this state-of-the-art science museum, named after the great Pisa-born scientist Galileo Galilei, who was invited by the Medici court to Florence in 1610. Don't miss two of his fingers and a tooth displayed here. (☏055 26 53 11;

www.museogalileo.it; Piazza dei Giudici 1; adult/reduced €10/6; ⊙9.30am-6pm Wed-Mon, to 1pm Tue)

Eating

Irene
BISTRO €€€

9 🍴 MAP P50, C3

Named after the accomplished Italian grandmother of Sir Rocco Forte of the eponymous luxury hotel group, Irene (part of neighbouring Hotel Savoy) is a dazzling contemporary bistro with a pavement terrace (heated in winter) overlooking iconic Piazza della Repubblica. Interior design is retro-chic 1950s and celebrity chef Fulvio Pierangelini cooks up playful, utterly fabulous bistro cuisine. (☎055 273 58 91; www.roccoforte hotels.com; Piazza della Repubblica 7; meals €60; ⊙7.30am-10.30pm)

Osteria I Buongustai
OSTERIA €

10 🍴 MAP P50, E4

Run with breathtaking speed and grace by Laura and Lucia, 'The Gourmand' is unmissable. Lunchtimes heave with locals and savvy students who flock here to fill up on tasty Tuscan home cooking at a fraction of other restaurant prices. The place is brilliantly no frills – watch women in hair caps at work in the kitchen, share a table and pay in cash. No credit cards. (☎055 29 13 04; www.facebook.com/ibuongustaifirenze; Via dei Cerchi 15r; meals €15-20; ⊙9.30am-3.30pm Mon-Sat)

Trattoria Le Mossacce
TRATTORIA €

11 🍴 MAP P50, F3

Strung with legs of ham and garlic garlands, this old-world trattoria lives up to its vintage promise of a warm *benvenuto* (welcome) and fabulous home cooking every Tuscan *nonna* would approve of. A family address, it has been the pride and joy of the Fantoni-Mannucci family for the last 50-odd years and their *bistecca alla fiorentina* (T-bone steak) is among the best in town. (☎055 29 43 61; www.trattorialemossacce.it; Via del Proconsolo 55r; meals €20; ⊙noon-2.30pm & 7-9.30pm Mon-Fri)

A classy Passeggiata

Nothing is more sacrosanct than the early-evening stroll; follow Florentines to **Via de' Tornabuoni**, the city's most expensive shopping strip nicknamed the 'Salotto di Firenze' (Florence's Drawing Room). Renaissance palaces and Italian fashion houses border each side of the elegant, car-free strip, making it prime terrain to don suitable dress and walk, chat and smooch in chic company. End with a bite-sized truffle *panini* and flute of sparkling prosecco at 19th-century English pharmacy-turned-genteel cafe Procacci (p59).

Backstreet Florence: Dante Alighieri

Italy's most divine poet was born in 1265 in a wee house down a narrow lane in the backstreets of Florence. Tragic romance made him tick and there's no better place to unravel the medieval life and times of Dante than the **Museo Casa di Dante** (🎣055 21 94 16; www. museocasadidante.it; Via Santa Margherita 1; adult/reduced €4/2; 🕙10am-6pm summer, 10am-5pm Mon-Fri, to 6pm Sat & Sun winter).

When Dante was just 12 he was promised in marriage to Gemma Donati. But it was another Florentine gal, Beatrice Portinari (1266–90), who was his muse, his inspiration, the love of his life (despite only ever meeting her twice in his life).

Beatrice, who wed a banker and died a couple of years later aged just 24, is buried in 11th-century **Chiesa di Santa Margherita** (Via Santa Margherita 4; 🕙hours vary), in an alley near Dante's house; note the wicker basket in front of her grave filled with scraps of paper on which prayers and dedications evoking unrequited love have been penned. This chapel was also where the poet married Gemma in 1295. Dimly lit, it remains much as it was in medieval Florence.

'Ino

SANDWICHES €

12 ✖️ MAP P50, D7

Artisan ingredients sourced locally and mixed creatively by passionate gourmet Alessandro Frassica are the secret behind this sandwich bar near the Uffizi. Create your own *panino* combo; pick from dozens of house specials; or go for an enticingly topped bruschetta – in the company of a glass of Tuscan wine or craft beer. (🎣055 21 45 14; www.inofirenze.com; Via dei Georgofili 3r-7r; panini €6-10; 🕙noon-4.30pm)

Grom

GELATO €

13 ✖️ MAP P50, D2

Rain, hail or shine, queues run halfway down the street at this sweet address that many say makes some of the best gelato in the city. Ingredients are organic and its tasty hot chocolate is a delicious winter warmer. (🎣055 21 61 58; www.grom.it; Via del Campanile 2; cones & tubs €2.60-5.50; 🕙10am-midnight Sun-Fri, to 1am Sat summer, 10.30am-10.30pm winter)

Cantinetta dei Verrazzano

TUSCAN €

14 ✖️ MAP P50, D4

A *forno* (baker's oven) and *cantinetta* (small cellar) make a heavenly match in foodie Florence. Sit down at a marble-topped table, sip your pick of wine from the Verrazzano family's 52-hectare estate in Greve in Chianti, and tuck into traditional focaccia, *cecina* (chickpea bread) or a mixed salami platter – the *sbriciolona* (fennel seed salami) is not to be missed. (☑ 055 26 85 90; www.verrazzano.com; Via dei Tavolini 18-20; snacks €3-8; ⏱ 8am-9pm Mon-Sat, 10am-9pm Sun summer, to 4.30pm Mon-Sat, to 5pm Sun winter)

Mangiafoco
TUSCAN €€

15 ✖ MAP P50, B6

Aromatic truffles get full-page billing at this small and cosy *osteria* with buttercup-yellow walls, cushioned seating and an exceptional wine list. Whether you are a hard-core truffle fiend or a truffle virgin, there is something for you here: steak topped with freshly shaved truffles in season, truffle *tagliatelle* (ribbon pasta) or a simple plate of mixed cheeses with sweet truffle honey. (☑ 055 265 81 70; www.mangiafoco.com; Borgo SS Apostoli 26r; meals €40; ⏱ noon-midnight)

Obicà
ITALIAN €€

16 ✖ MAP P50, A3

Given its exclusive location in Palazzo Tornabuoni, this designer address is naturally ubertrendy – even the table mats are upcycled from organic products. Taste 10 different types of mozzarella cheese in the cathedral-like interior or snuggle beneath heaters over pizza and salads on sofas in the enchanting star-topped courtyard. At *aperitivo* hour, nibble on *taglierini* (tasting boards loaded with cheeses, salami and deep-fried veg). (☑ 055 277 35 26; www.obica.com; Via de' Tornabuoni 16; meals

Traditional Tripe Carts 🍽

When Florentines fancy a munch-on-the-move, they flit by a *trippaio* – a cart on wheels or mobile stand – for a tripe *panini*. Think cow's stomach chopped up, boiled, sliced, seasoned and bunged between bread.

Those great bastions of good old-fashioned Florentine tradition still going strong include **Il Trippaio del Porcellino** (☑ 335 8070240; Piazza del Mercato Nuovo 1; tripe €4.50; ⏱ 9am-6.30pm Mon-Sat) and hole-in-the-wall **Da Vinattieri** (www.facebook.com/davinattieri; Via Santa Margherita 4; panini €4.50; ⏱ 11.30am-7pm). Pay €4.50 for a *panini* with tripe doused in *salsa verde* (pea-green sauce of smashed parsley, garlic, capers and anchovies) or order a bowl of *lampredotto* (cow's fourth stomach, chopped and simmered).

€30-50; ⏱ noon-4pm & 6.30-11.30pm Mon-Fri, noon-11pm Sat & Sun)

Drinking

La Terrazza Lounge Bar
BAR

17 🍷 MAP P50, C6

This rooftop bar with a wood-decked terrace accessible from the 5th floor of the Hotel Continentale is as chic as one would

The Finest Ice in Town

Known throughout Italy for the quality of its handmade gelato and sweet pastries, **Gelateria Pasticceria Badiani** (☑055 57 86 82; www.buontalenti.it; Viale dei Mille 20r; ☉7am-1am summer, to midnight Sun-Thu, to 1am Fri & Sat winter) is located in the Campo de' Marte neighbourhood just outside the historic city centre but is – as any local will tell you – well worth the walk. The house speciality is Buontalenti gelato, a creamy concoction with flavourings that are a heavily guarded house secret.

expect of a fashion-house hotel. Its *aperitivo* buffet is a modest affair (simple nuts and juicy olives), but who cares with that gorgeous panorama of Florence. Dress the part, or feel out of place. Count on around €20 for a cocktail. (☑055 2726 5987, 342 1234710; www. lungarnocollection.com; Vicolo dell'Oro 6r; ☉3.30-10.30pm Apr-Sep)

Mayday Club   COCKTAIL BAR

18 🚇 MAP P50, E4

Strike up a conversation with passionate mixologist Marco Arduino at Mayday. Within seconds you'll be hooked on his mixers and astonishing infusions, all handmade using wholly Tuscan ingredients. Think artichoke- and thistle-infused vermouth, pancetta

whisky and porcini liqueur. Marco's cocktail list is equally impressive – or tell him your favourite flavours and let yourself be surprised. (☑055 238 12 90; www.maydayclub.it; Via Dante Alighieri 16; cocktails €8-10; ☉8pm-2am Tue-Sat)

Caffè Gilli   CAFE

19 🚇 MAP P50, C3

Popular with locals who sip coffee standing up at the long marble bar, this is the most famous of the historic cafes on the city's old Roman forum. Gilli has been serving delectable cakes, chocolates, fruit tartlets and *millefoglie* (lighter-than-light vanilla or custard slice) since 1733. It moved to this square in 1910 and has a beautifully preserved art-nouveau interior.

Don't be surprised to pay three times as much for a drink sitting down – either inside or in the conservatory-style, glassed-in terrace with prime square view – rather than at the bar; a cappuccino costs €1.40 standing up and €5.50 when served at a table. (☑055 21 38 96; www.gilli.it; Piazza della Repubblica 39r; ☉7.30am-1am)

Amblé   BAR

20 🚇 MAP P50, B6

'Fresh food and old furniture' is the catchy strapline of this cafe-bar hidden in an alleyway near Ponte Vecchio. Vintage furniture – all for sale – creates a shabby-chic vibe and the tiny terrace feels delightfully far from the madding crowd on summer evenings. From the river, follow Vicolo dell'Oro to Hotel Continentale, then turn left along the alley running parallel to the river. (☏055 26 85 28; www.amble.it; Piazzetta dei Del Bene 7a; ◷10am-midnight Tue-Sat, from noon Sun)

Coquinarius   WINE BAR

21 🚇 MAP P50, E3

With its old stone vaults, scrubbed wooden tables and modern air, this *enoteca* run by the dynamic Nicolas is spacious and stylish. The wine list features bags of Tuscan greats and unknowns, and outstanding crostini and *carpacci* (cold sliced meats) ensure you don't leave hungry.

The pear-accompanied cheese ravioli and *raviolotti* stuffed with silky burrata cheese and smoth-ered in pistachio pesto are both sensational. (☏055 230 21 53; www.coquinarius.com; Via delle Oche 11r; ◷12.30-3pm & 6.30-10.30pm Wed-Mon)

Procacci   CAFE

22 🚇 MAP P50, A3

The last remaining bastion of genteel old Florence on Via de' Tornabuoni, this tiny cafe was born in 1885 as a delicatessen serving truffles in its repertoire of tasty morsels. Bite-sized *panini tartufati* (truffle-pâté rolls) remain the thing to order, best accompanied by a glass of prosecco. (☏055 21 16 56; www.procacci1885.it; Via de' Tornabuoni 64r; ◷10am-9pm Mon-Sat, 11am-8pm Sun, closed 3 weeks Aug)

Fiaschetteria Nuvoli   WINE BAR

23 🚇 MAP P50, C1

Pull up a stool on the street and chat with a regular over a glass of *vino della casa* (house wine) at this old-fashioned *fiaschetteria* (wine seller), a street away from the *duomo*. Food too. (☏055 239 66 16; Piazza dell'Olio 15r; ◷8am-9pm Mon-Sat)

Shake Café   CAFE

24 🚇 MAP P50, E3

Smoothie bowls with protein powder, kale and goji berries, cold-pressed juices and vitamin-packed elixir shots – to eat in or take away – satisfy wellness cravings at this laid-back cafe on people-busy Via del Corso. International newspa-pers, mellow music and a relaxed vibe make it a hipster place to hang. All-day wraps, salads and hearty, homemade soups (€6 to €8) too. (☏055 21 59 52; www.shakecafe.bio; Via del Corso 28-32; ◷7.30am-8pm)

Aperitivi Destinations

Join locals for summertime early-evening cocktails on the chic rooftop terrace of La Terrazza Lounge Bar (p57) or the back-alley garden of shabby-chic Amblé. Winter or summer, stylish Irene (p55), with a box terrace on Piazza della Repubblica, is an *aperi-tivo* hot spot.

Florentine Artists

In many respects, the history of Florentine art is also the history of Western art. Browse through any text on the subject and you'll quickly develop an understanding of how influential the Italian Renaissance, which kicked off and reached its greatest flowering here, has been over the past 500 years. Indeed, it's no exaggeration to say that architecture, painting and sculpture rely on its technical innovations and take inspiration from its humanist subject matter to this very day.

Of the many artists who trained, worked and lived in the city, the most famous are Giotto di Bondone (c 1266–1337), Donatello (c 1386–1466), Fra' Angelico (c 1395–1455), Masaccio (1401–28), Filippo Lippi (c 1406–69), Benozzo Gozzoli (c 1421–97), Sandro Botticelli (1445–1510), Domenico Ghirlandaio (1449–94) and Michelangelo Buonarroti (1475–1564).

The city is full of artistic masterpieces – in fact, Florence itself is often described as the world's biggest and most spectacular museum. It's impossible to see everything in one trip, but the **Uffizi Gallery** should be every visitor's first stop. Its peerless collection contains major works by every Renaissance artist of note, with Botticelli's *Primavera*, *Birth of Venus*, *Cestello Annunciation* and *Adoration of the Magi* being four of the gallery's best-loved works (Michelangelo's *Tondo Doni* is another).

Sculptures abound – most notably Michelangelo's *David* in the **Galleria dell'Accademia** – but the greatest and most significant concentration of works can be found in the **Museo del Bargello**, home to Donatello's two versions of *David* (one marble, the other bronze) and a number of works by Michelangelo.

Frescoing was an important artistic technique in the Renaissance, and Florentine churches are rich repositories of these murals painted on freshly laid lime plaster. Head to **Basilica di Santa Maria Novella** to see Ghirlandaio's wonderful examples in the Cappella Maggiore; the **Museo di San Marco** to see those of Fra' Angelico (including his deeply spiritual *Annunciation*); the **Cappella Brancacci** to see Masaccio's oft-reproduced *Expulsion of Adam and Eve from Paradise;* and the **Palazzo Medici-Riccardi** to admire Benozzo Gozzoli's charming *Procession of the Magi to Bethlehem*.

YAB
CLUB

25 MAP P50, B4

Pick your night according to your age and tastes – disco, rock 'n' roll, groove or a 'UnYversal' bit of everything – at this hugely popular nightclub with electric dance floor, around since the 1970s, behind Palazzo Strozzi. (055 21 51 60; www.yab.it/en; Via de' Sassetti 5r; 7pm-4am Mon & Wed-Sat Oct-May)

Shopping

A Piedi Nudi nel Parco
FASHION & ACCESSORIES

26 MAP P50, F4

With a name meaning 'Barefoot in the Park', this boutique specialising in high-end avant-garde fashion for women is hard to resist. So chic, it has a part-transparent floor exposing the building's ancient foundations below and a tiny bar serving *aperitivi* (from 6pm) while you shop. Find its equally funky **men's store** (055 28 01 79; 10.30am-7.30pm Mon-Sat, 11am-8pm Sun) just around the corner on Via Santa Margherita. (055 21 80 99; www.pnp-firenze.com; Via del Proconsolo 1; 10.30am-7.30pm Mon-Sat, 11am-8pm Sun)

Boutique Nadine
FASHION & ACCESSORIES

27 MAP P50, B6

For exquisite vintage clothing, jewellery and stylish knick-knacks for the home curated by inquisitive travellers and Florentines Irene and partner Matteo, browse this old-world boutique on the riverside near Ponte Vecchio. Look out for Irene's own label, Odette, embracing romantic print dresses evocative of old-world Florence. You'll find a second branch (p105) in Santa Croce. (055 28 78 51; www.boutiquenadine.com; Lungarno degli Acciaiuoli 22r; 10am-7.30pm Mon-Sat, to 7pm Sun)

Patrizia Pepe
FASHION & ACCESSORIES

28 MAP P50, C2

Modern, colourful designs for women and children are the signature of this Florentine fashion house, created in 1993 by creative spirit Patrizia Bambi and business partner Claudio Orrea. A bit rock chic, a bit wild child, Patrizia Pepe never fails to thrill. (055 264 50 56; www.patriziapepe.com; Piazza di San Giovanni 12r; 9am-8pm)

La Bottega dell'Olio
FOOD

29 MAP P50, B6

This bijou boutique takes great care with its displays of olive oils, olive-oil soaps, platters made from olive wood and skincare products made with olive oil (the Lepo range is particularly good). (055 267 04 68; www.labottegadelliofirenze.it; Piazza del Limbo 4r; 2.30-6.30pm Mon, 10am-1pm & 2-6.30pm Tue-Sat)

Explore ⊕
Santa Maria Novella

Anchored by its magnificent basilica, this ancient and intriguing part of Florence defies easy description – from the rough-cut streets around the station it's only a short walk to the busy social scene around recently gentrified Piazza di Santa Maria Novella and the hip boutiques on the atmosphere-laden 'backstreets' west of elegant Via de' Tornabuoni.

The Short List

○ **Basilica di Santa Maria Novella (p64)** *Marvelling at exquisite Renaissance frescoes in sacred serenity.*

○ **Officina Profumo-Farmaceutica di Santa Maria Novella (p73)** *Shopping for old-fashioned scents, beauty potions and herbal remedies conceived by Dominican friars in the 17th century.*

○ **Benheart (p72)** *Slipping your feet in silky soft, hand-made leather shoes crafted by one of Florence's finest contemporary artisans.*

○ **Museo Novecento (p68)** *Escaping the Renaissance with an inspirational dose of eye-catching, early-20th-century Italian art.*

○ **Museo Marino Marini (p68)** *Setting out to admire modern Tuscan sculptures and stumbling upon a breathtaking miniature of Christ's Holy Sepulchre in Jerusalem.*

Getting There

🚶 From Piazza della Stazione turn south into Via degli Avelli and you will almost immediately come to Piazza di Santa Maria Novella and its magnificent basilica.

Santa Maria Novella Map on p66

Basilica di Santa Maria Novella (p64) SILVERFOX999/SHUTTERSTOCK ©

Top Experience 📷
Wander the Basilica di Santa Maria Novella

This monastery complex, fronted by the mesmerising green-and-white marble facade of its basilica, hides serene church cloisters and stunning frescoed chapels behind its monumental walls. The basilica safeguards several artistic masterpieces, including breathtaking frescoes by Domenico Ghirlandaio and a luminous painted Crucifix by Giotto (c 1290).

◎ MAP P66, G3

📞 055 21 92 57

www.smn.it

adult/reduced €7.50/5

🕐 9am-7pm Mon-Thu, 11am-7pm Fri, 9am-6.30pm Sat, noon-6.30pm Sun Jul & Aug, shorter hours rest of year

Holy Trinity

Upon entering the church, admire Masaccio's superb fresco *Trinità* (Holy Trinity; 1424–25), one of the first artworks to use the newly discovered techniques of perspective and proportion.

Cappella Maggiore

Look behind the main altar to find this tiny chapel adorned in vibrant frescoes by Ghirlandaio between 1485 and 1490. Relating the lives of the Virgin Mary, the frescoes are notable for their depiction of Florentine life during the Renaissance. Spot portraits of the Tornabuoni family who commissioned the frescoes.

Cappella Strozzi di Mantova

To the far left of the altar, up a short flight of stairs, is this wonderful chapel covered in soul-stirring 14th-century frescoes by Niccolò di Tommaso and Nardo di Cione. The fine altarpiece (1354–57) here was painted by the latter's brother, Andrea, best known as Andrea Orcagna.

Chiostro Verde

The serenely beautiful Green Cloister (1332–62) is named after the green earth base used for the frescoes on three of its four walls. On its west side, another passage leads to 14th-century **Cappella degli Ubriachi** and a refectory (1353–54) featuring ecclesiastical relics and a 1583 *Last Supper* by Alessandro Allori.

Cappellone degli Spagnoli

A door off the cloister's northern side leads into this chapel, named in 1566 when it was given to the Spanish colony in Florence (Spagnoli means Spanish). Its extraordinary frescoes (c 1365–67) by Andrea di Bonaiuto depict the *Resurrection*, *Ascension* and *Pentecost* (vault); on the altar wall are scenes of the *Via Dolorosa*, *Crucifixion* and *Descent into Limbo*. Spot portraits of Giotto, Boccaccio, Petrarch and Dante in *The Militant and Triumphant Church* (pictured).

★ Top Tips

o Allow at least two hours to take it all in; book highly recommended guided tours (€4, 1¼ hours) through Muse Firenze (p54) or directly at the museum.

✕ Take a Break

Freshen up with a herbal infusion at Officina Profumo-Farmaceutica di Santa Maria Novella (p73), a 17th-century pharmacy-boutique with tea-room where monks from Santa Maria Novella concocted herbal remedies in the 17th century.

The marble steps leading up to the basilica are a sun trap: grab a drink and a bespoke *panino* from Mariano (p70).

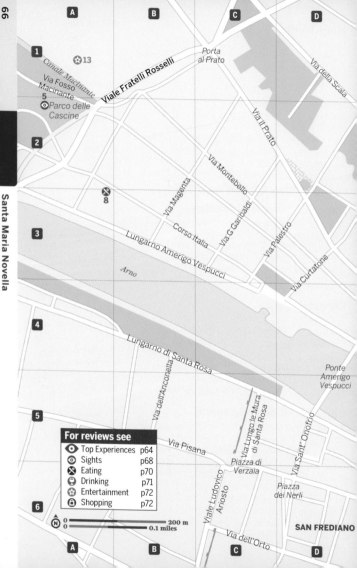

A B C D

1

☆13

Canale Macinante

Porta al Prato

Via della Scala

Via Fosso Macinante

5

◉ Parco delle Cascine

Viale Fratelli Rosselli

Via Il Prato

2

Via Montebello

Via Magenta

Via G Garibaldi

✖
8

Via Palestro

3

Corso Italia

Lungarno Amerigo Vespucci

Via Curtatone

Arno

4

Lungarno di Santa Rosa

Ponte Amerigo Vespucci

Via dell'Anconella

5

Via Lungo le Mura di Santa Rosa

Via Sant'Onofrio

Via Pisana

Piazza di Verzaia

Piazza dei Nerli

For reviews see

◉ Top Experiences p64
◉ Sights p68
✖ Eating p70
◓ Drinking p71
☆ Entertainment p72
🔒 Shopping p72

6

Ⓝ 0 ___ 200 m
0 ___ 0.1 miles

Viale Ludovico Ariosto

Via dell'Orto

SAN FREDIANO

A B C D

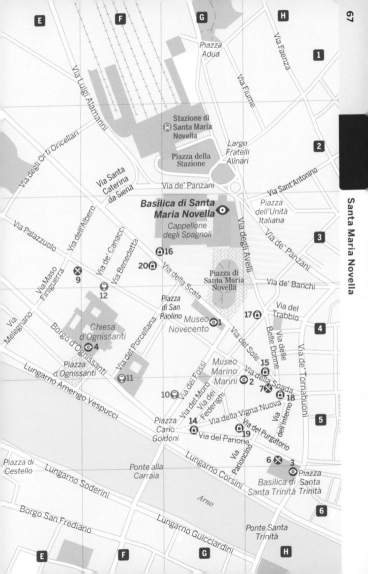

E F G H

1

Via Faenza

Piazza Adua

Via Fiume

Via Luigi Alamanni

Stazione di Santa Maria Novella

Largo Fratelli Alinari

2

Piazza della Stazione

Via Sant'Antonino

Via de' Panzani

Piazza dell'Unità Italiana

Via Santa Caterina da Siena

Via degli Or ti Oricellari

Basilica di Santa Maria Novella ◉

Via de' Panzani

3

Via Palazzuolo

Cappellone degli Spagnoli

Via degli Avelli

Via de' Banchi

Via dell'Albero

Via de' Canacci

16 🏛

Via Benedetta

20 🔒

Via della Scala

Piazza di Santa Maria Novella

Via del Trabbio

Via Maso Finiguerra

9 🍴

12 🍷

Piazza di San Paolino

Museo Novecento 1 ◉

17 🔒

Via delle Belle Donne

Via del Sole

Via del Fossi

Via della Spada

Via della Spada

15 🍷

Via di Tornabuoni

Via Melegnano

Chiesa d'Ognissanti

Borgo d'Ognissanti

4 ◉

Via del Porcellana

Museo Marino Marini 2 ◉

7 🍴

18

Piazza d'Ognissanti

11 🍷

Lungarno Amerigo Vespucci

10 🍴

Via del Moro

Via dei Federighi

Via della Vigna Nuova

Via dell'Inferno

5

Piazza di Cestello

Piazza Carlo Goldoni

14 🔒

19

Via del Purgatorio

Via del Parione

Via del Pariondino

Via Pandino

6 🍴 3

Ponte alla Carraia

Lungarno Corsini

6 ◉ Piazza Santa Trinità

Basilica di Santa Trinità

Lungarno Soderini

Arno

6

Borgo San Frediano

Lungarno Guicciardini

Ponte Santa Trinità

E F G H

Florentine Street Art

Take a break from Renaissance art at **Street Levels Gallery** (☎339 2203607; https://street-level-gallery. business.site; Via Palazzuolo 74r; ⏰3-7pm Tue-Sat), a pioneering urban street-art gallery showcasing the work of urban street artists. These include street-sign hacker Clet (p125); the stencil art of Hogre; and ExitEnter, whose work is easily recognisable by the red balloons holding up the matchstick figures he draws. A highlight is the enigmatic Blub, whose caricatures of historical figures wearing goggles and diving masks adorn many a city wall – his art is known as *L'Arte Sa Nuotare* (Art Knows how to Swim). Check the gallery's Facebook page for workshops, cultural events, *aperitivi* (evening drinks) and other uber-cool happenings.

Sights

Museo Novecento
MUSEUM

1 ◉ **MAP P66, G4**

Don't allow the Renaissance to distract you from Florence's fantastic modern art museum, at home in a 13th-century pilgrim shelter, hospital and school. A well-articulated itinerary guides visitors through modern Italian painting and sculpture from the early 20th century to the late 1980s. Installation art makes effective use of the outside space on the 1st-floor loggia. Fashion and theatre also get a nod, and the itinerary ends with a 20-minute cinematic montage of the best films set in Florence. (Museum of the 20th Century; ☎055 28 61 32; www.museonovecento.it; Piazza di Santa Maria Novella 10; adult/reduced €9.50/4.50; ⏰11am-8pm Sat-Wed, to 2pm Thu, to 11pm Fri summer, 11am-7pm Fri-Wed, to 2pm Thu winter)

Museo Marino Marini
GALLERY

2 ◉ **MAP P66, H5**

Deconsecrated in the 19th century, Chiesa di San Pancrazio is home to this small art museum displaying sculptures by Pistoia-born sculptor Marino Marini (1901–80) intertwined with various contemporary art exhibits (free admission). But the highlight is **Cappella Rucellai** with a tiny scale copy of Christ's Holy Sepulchre in Jerusalem – a Renaissance gem by Leon Battista Alberti. The chapel was built between 1458 and 1467 for the tomb of wealthy Florentine banker and wool merchant Giovanni Rucellai. (☎055 21 94 32; www.museomarino marini.it; Piazza San Pancrazio 1; chapel adult/reduced €6/4; ⏰10am-7pm Sat-Mon, by online reservation only Tue-Fri)

Basilica di Santa Trinità

CHURCH

3 ⊙ MAP P66, H6

Built in Gothic style and later given a mannerist facade, this 14th-century church shelters some of the city's finest frescoes. Right of the main altar, paintings (1483–85) by Ghirlandaio depict the life of St Francis of Assisi through portraits of illustrious Florentines of the time in **Cappella Sassetti**, (pop €0.50 in the slot to illuminate the frescoes). In **Cappella Bartholini Salimbeni**, the gated side chapel, Lorenzo Monaco's *Annunciation* (1422) sits above the altar and wall frescoes illustrate the life of the Virgin Mary. (Piazza Santa Trinità; admission free; ⊙7am-noon & 4-7pm)

Chiesa d'Ognissanti

CHURCH

4 ⊙ MAP P66, F4

Stroll along Borgo d'Ognissanti from Piazza Carlo Goldoni towards ancient city gate Porta al Prato, past antiques shops and designer boutiques, to reach this 13th-century church, built as part of a Benedictine monastery. Its highlight is Domenico Ghirlandaio's fresco of the Madonna della Misericordia protecting members of the Vespucci family, the church's main patrons. Amerigo Vespucci, the Florentine navigator who gave his name to the American continent, is supposed to be the young boy whose head peeks between the Madonna and the old man. (📞055 239 87 00; Borgo d'Ognissanti 42; admission free;

Santa Maria Novella Sights

Chiesa d'Ognissanti

Botticelli Essential

Having exhausted the masterpieces in the Uffizi Gallery, there is another essential stop for Botticelli aficionados: the early Renaissance artist's grave inside Chiesa d'Ognissanti (p69). The artist had requested to be buried at the feet of Simonetta Vespucci, the married woman whom Botticelli was said to be in love with and who served as a model for one of his greatest masterpieces, *Primavera* (*Spring*). Look for the simple round tombstone marked 'Sandro Filipepe' in the south transept. Botticelli grew up in a house on the same street and a pensive St Augustine, painted by him in 1480, hangs in the church.

⏱9.30am-12.30pm & 4-6pm Mon-Sat, 9-10am & 4-5.30pm Sun)

Parco delle Cascine

PARK

5 ◉ MAP P66, A2

Florence's largest park is dotted with playgrounds and is a great place to let the little 'uns loose. Families take over at weekends and the park is a colourful scene with rollerbladers, kite-flyers, joggers and kids on bikes. In summer you can also use Le Pavoniere swimming pool. (Viale degli Olmi)

Eating

Mariano

SANDWICHES €

6 ✖ MAP P66, H5

A local favourite for its simplicity and correct prices, around since 1973. From sunrise to sunset, this brick-vaulted, 13th-century cellar gently buzzes with Florentines propped at the counter sipping coffee or wine or eating salads and *panini*. Come here for a coffee-and-pastry breakfast, light lunch, an *aperitivo* with cheese or salami tasting platter (€13 to €17), or a *panino* to eat on the move. (☎055 21 40 67; Via del Parione 19r; panini €3.50-6; ⏱8am-3pm & 5-7.30pm Mon-Fri, 8am-3pm Sat)

Trattoria Marione

TRATTORIA €€

7 ✖ MAP P66, H5

For the quintessential 'Italian dining' experience, Marione is gold. It's busy, it's noisy, it's 99.9% local and the cuisine is right out of *nonna*'s Tuscan kitchen. No one appears to speak English so go for Italian – the tasty excellent-value traditional fare is worth it. If you don't get a complimentary *limoncello* (lemon liqueur) with the bill, you clearly failed the language test. (☎055 21 47 56; Via della Spada 27; meals €30; ⏱noon-5pm & 7-11pm)

Borderline
TUSCAN €€

8 ✗ MAP P66, A3

From the team behind San Marco's iconic Antica Trattoria da Tito (p89; around since 1913), Borderline is a stylish advocate of Tuscan culinary tradition. Inside a former theatre, it serves classic artichokes and wild boar pasta, alongside creative fish dishes like seafood *ribollita* (Tuscan bread soup) and homemade *pici* pasta with mussels, black pepper and cheese, to a staunchly local crowd. (☎055 28 87 71; www.borderline-firenze.com; Corso Italia 35; meals €35; ☺noon-3pm & 7.30pm-midnight Mon-Fri, 7.30pm-midnight Sat)

Il Contadino
TRATTORIA €

9 ✗ MAP P66, E3

Come the weekend, this no-frills trattoria gets packed with families lunching with gusto on its astonishingly good-value Tuscan cuisine. Lunch, moreover, is served until 3.30pm, when the dinner menu kicks in, meaning convenient all-day dining. The day's menu includes 10 or so dishes, including meaty classics like roast rabbit, tripe and oven-roasted pork shank. Two-course lunch/dinner menus start at €10/14. (☎055 238 26 73; www.trattoriailcontadino.com; Via Palazzuolo 69-71r; meals €10-22; ☺noon-10.30pm)

Drinking

Todo Modo
CAFE

10 ☕ MAP P66, G5

An exceptional range of books (new and old, Italian and English), curated with care and impeccable taste by savvy owners Pietro and Maddalena, promise hours of browsing at this world-class independent bookshop-cafe. A fashionable cafe–wine bar – the perfect lunch date – and a catchy repertoire of book readings and other cultural soirées hosted in its pocket theatre only adds to the undeniable hipster allure. (☎055 239 91 10; www.todomodo.org; Via dei Fossi 15r; ☺10am-8pm Tue-Sun, closed Sun May-Sep)

Santa Maria Novella Drinking

Cheap Romance

Before sunset, follow the lead of savvy, budget-conscious Florentines: buy a bottle of wine and head to the hottest seats in town – the smooth, stone platform created by the east-facing bridge supports of **Ponte Santa Trìnita**. Sit above the swirling water and toast the sun as it sinks behind the romantic, star-lit Ponte Vecchio further down the river.

Picnic Perfect 🍽

Follow the trail of knowing Florentines, past the flower- and veg-laden bicycle parked outside, into **La Bottega Della Frutta** (☎055 239 85 90; Via dei Federighi 31r; ⏰8.30am-7.30pm Mon-Sat, closed Aug), an enticing food shop bursting with boutique cheeses, organic fruit and veg, biscuits, chocolates, conserved produce, excellent-value wine et al. Mozzarella oozing raw milk arrives fresh from Eboli in Sicily every Tuesday, and if you're looking to buy olive oil, this is the place to taste. Simply ask Elisabeta or her husband, Francesco.

Sei Divino   WINE BAR

11 🟢 MAP P66, F4

This stylish wine bar tucked beneath a red-brick vaulted ceiling is a veteran on Florence's prolific wine-bar scene. Come here for music and occasional exhibitions as well as fine wine. *Aperitivi* 'hour' (with copious banquet) runs from 7pm to 10pm, with a buoyant crowd spilling outside onto the pavement in summer. (☎055 21 57 94; Borgo d'Ognissanti 42r; ⏰6pm-1am Wed-Mon)

Space Club   CLUB

12 🟢 MAP P66, F4

Sheer size at this vast nightclub in Santa Maria Novella impresses –

dancing, drinking, video-karaoke in the bar, and a mixed student-international crowd.

Keep tally of how many drinks you consume: drinks are clocked up on a tab, and paid for before leaving. Entrance can be anything from free to €18 including one drink. (☎055 29 30 82; www.facebook.com/spacefirenze2; Via Palazzuolo 37r; admission variable; ⏰10pm-3am Sun-Tue & Thu, to 4am Fri, to 4.30am Sat)

Entertainment

Teatro del Maggio Musicale Fiorentino   PERFORMING ARTS

13 ⭐ MAP P66, A1

This strikingly modern theatre with glittering contemporary geometric facade sits on the green edge of city park Parco delle Cascine. Its three thoughtfully designed and multifunctional concert halls can seat an audience of 5000 in total and play host to opera, theatre, ballet, dance and classical-music performances. Come springtime, the curtain rises on the **Maggio Musicale Fiorentino** (www.maggiofiorentino.com; ⏰Apr-Jun). (☎055 200 12 78; www.maggiofiorentino.com; Piazzale Vittorio Gui 1; ⏰box office 10am-6pm Mon-Sat)

Shopping

Benheart   FASHION & ACCESSORIES

14 🔵 MAP P66, G5

Evocative of an artisan workshop, this tiny boutique showcases the world-class leather craft of local superstar Benheart. The young Florentine fashion designer went into business with schoolmate Matteo after undergoing a heart transplant. The pair swore that if Ben survived, they would set up shop on their own. Their hand-made shoes (from €190), for men and women, are among the finest in Florence. (☑055 239 94 83; www. benheart.it; Via della Vigna Nuova 95-97r; ◷9am-8pm)

Mio Concept HOMEWARES

15 🔒 MAP P66, H4

Design objects for the home – made in Italy and many upcycled – as well as jewellery, bags and belts crafted from old bicycle tyres and inner tubes by Turinese designers

Cingomma, and so on, cram this stylish boutique created by Ger-man globetrotter Antje. Don't miss the prints of iconic designs by Italian street artists Blub and Exit Enter, and street-sign artworks by Florence's Clet (p125).

Limited-edition street signs, of which Clet produces just 13 of each design, start at several thousand euros. (☑055 264 55 43; www.mio-concept.com; Via della Spada 34r; ◷10am-1.30pm & 2.30-7.30pm Mon-Sat)

Officina Profumo-Farmaceutica di Santa Maria Novella GIFTS

16 🔒 MAP P66, F3

In business since 1612, this exqui-site perfumery-pharmacy began

Officina Profumo-Farmaceutica di Santa Maria Novella

PETE SEAWARD/LONELY PLANET ©

life when Santa Maria Novella's Dominican friars began to concoct cures and sweet-smelling unguents using medicinal herbs cultivated in the monastery garden. The shop, with an interior from 1848, sells fragrances, skincare products, ancient herbal remedies and preparations for everything from relief of heavy legs to improving skin elasticity, memory and mental energy. (☎055 21 62 76; www.smnovella.it; Via della Scala 16; ☺9am-8pm)

Aprosio & Co FASHION & ACCESSORIES

17 🅐 MAP P66, H4

Ornella Aprosio fashions teeny-tiny Murano glass and crystal beads into dazzling pieces of jewellery, hair accessories, animal-shaped brooches, handbags, even glass-flecked cashmere. It is all quite magical. (☎055 21 01 27; www.aprosio.it; Via del Moro 75-77r; ☺10.30am-6.30pm Mon-Sat)

Grevi FASHION & ACCESSORIES

18 🅐 MAP P66, H5

It was a hat made by Siena milliner Grevi that actress Cher wore in the film *Tea with Mussolini* (1999); ditto Maggie Smith in *My House in Umbria* (2003). So if you want to shop like a star for a hat by Grevi, this hopelessly romantic boutique is the address. Hats range in price from €30 to possibly unaffordable. (☎055 26 41 39; www.grevi.it; Via della Spada 11-13r; ☺10am-2pm & 3-8pm Mon-Sat)

Pineider

JULIET COOMBE/LONELY PLANET ©

Pineider

ARTS & CRAFTS

19 🔒 MAP P66, G5

'Writing the Future' is the inspired strapline of this iconic stationery company, in business in Florence since 1714. Stendhal, Byron, Shelley and Dickens are among the literary luminaries who have chosen to purchase its beautifully crafted, top-quality paper products, pens and leather goods.

For a real treat, order your own bespoke writing paper. (📞055 28 46 56; www.pineider.com; Piazza de' Rucellai 4-7r; ⏰10am-7pm)

Dolceforte

CHOCOLATE

20 🔒 MAP P66, F3

Elena is the passion and knowledge behind this astonishing chocolate shop that sells only the best. Think black-truffle-flavoured chocolate, an entire cherry, stone and all, soaked in grappa and wrapped in white chocolate or –

Trainspotting in Florence

Most people rush through Florence's main train station, **Stazione di Santa Maria Novella** (www.firenzesantamaria novella.it; Piazza della Stazione), without a second glance, but in fact it's one of Italy's great modernist buildings. Built in the early 1930s, the station's plain facade mimics the rough stone of churches such as San Lorenzo, while the red-and-white striped marble floors recall the city's official colours.

for the ultimate taste sensation – *formaggio di fossa* (a cheese from central Italy) soaked in sweet wine and enrobed in dark chocolate. (📞055 21 91 16; www.dolceforte.it; Via della Scala 21; ⏰10am-1pm & 3.30-7.45pm Wed-Sat & Mon, 3.30-7.45pm Tue)

Explore ⊕
San Lorenzo &
San Marco

This part of the city fuses a gutsy market precinct – a covered produce market and noisy street stalls surrounding the Basilica di San Lorenzo – with Piazza San Marco, home to Florence University and a much-loved monastery museum. Between the two is the world's most famous sculpture, David. The result is a sensory experience with urban grit and uplifting art.

The Short List

o *Galleria dell'Accademia (p78)* Swooning over the world's most famous nude.

o *Museo di San Marco (p83)* Bathing in peace, tranquility and medieval cell art in Florence's most spiritual monastery museum.

o *Museo degli Innocenti (p84)* Learning the heart-tearing story behind Europe's oldest orphanage; post-visit rooftop drink obligatory.

o *Museo delle Cappelle Medicee (p82)* Savouring unsung Michelangelo sculptures in a gem-encrusted mausoleum for kings and queens.

o *Trattoria Mario (p86)* Sinking your teeth into a brilliantly blue bistecca alla fiorentina.

Getting There

🚶 From Piazza della Stazione walk southeast along Via de' Panzani and turn left (northeast) into Via del Giglio, which takes you to the Museo dell Cappelle Medicee, Piazza San Lorenzo and Basilica di San Lorenzo. Then walk east along Via de' Pucci and north into Via Ricasoli to reach the Galleria dell'Accademia and Piazza San Marco.

San Lorenzo & San Marco Map on p80

Street market, San Lorenzo SIMONA SIRIO/SHUTTERSTOCK ©

Top Experience 📷

Explore the Galleria dell'Accademia

A lengthy queue marks the door to this gallery, purpose-built to house one of the Renaissance's greatest masterpieces, Michelangelo's David. Fortunately, the world's most famous statue is worth the wait. Also here are Michelangelo's unfinished Prigioni sculpture and paintings by Andrea Orcagna, Taddeo Gaddi, Domenico Ghirlandaio, Filippino Lippi and Sandro Botticelli.

◉ MAP P80, E4

📞 055 098 71 00

www.galleriaaccademia
firenze.beniculturali.it

Via Ricasoli 58/60

adult/reduced €12/2

🕗 8.15am-6.50pm
Tue-Sun

Michelangelo's David

Carved from a single block of marble already worked on by two sculptors, Michelangelo's most famous work was challenging to complete. Yet the subtle detail of the enormous work of art – the veins in his sinewy arms, the leg muscles, the change in expression as you move around the statue – is indeed impressive. Thankfully for Michelangelo, when the statue of the nude boy-warrior – depicted for the first time as a man rather than a young boy – appeared on Piazza della Signoria in 1504, Florentines immediately adopted *David* as an emblem of power, liberty and civic pride.

The Slaves

Another soul-soaring work by Michelangelo, *Prigioni* (1521–30) evokes four 'prisoners' or 'slaves' so powerfully that the figures really do seem to be writhing and struggling to free themselves from the ice-cold marble. The work was intended for the tomb of Pope Julius II in Rome, which was never completed.

Coronation of the Virgin

This remarkable piece of embroidery – an altar frontal 4m long and over 1m wide – portrays the *Coronazione della Vergine* (Coronation of the Virgin; 1336) in exquisite detail using polychrome silks and gold and silver thread. Completed by master embroiderer Jacopo Cambi, it originally covered the high altar of the Basilica di Santa Maria Novella.

Botticelli's Madonna

Madonna del mare (Madonna of the Sea; 1477), a portrait of the Virgin and child by Sandro Botticelli, exudes a mesmerising serenity. Compare it with works in the gallery by Botticelli's master and mentor, Fra' Filippo Lippi (c 1457–1504), to whom some critics attribute it.

★ Top Tips

○ Book tickets in advance at Firenze Musei (p179): the reservation fee is €4.

○ Trail the world's best-known naked man around town: admire *David* copies on Piazza della Signoria and Piazzale Michelangelo; see Davids sculpted by other artists in Museo del Bargello.

○ Visit on the first Sunday of the month when admission is free.

✗ Take a Break

Keep cool in the queue with a gelato or almond *granita* (ice drink) from Sicilian-style ice-cream shop, Carabé (p89).

Grab a quick bite from Pugi bakery (p90), a favourite for pizza slices and *schiacciata* (Tuscan flatbread), spiked with salt and rosemary.

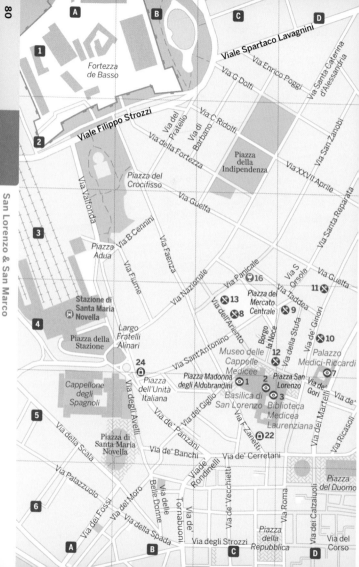

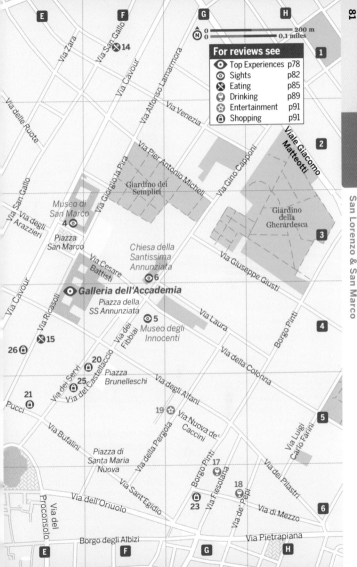

San Lorenzo & San Marco

For reviews see
- Top Experiences p78
- Sights p82
- Eating p85
- Drinking p89
- Entertainment p91
- Shopping p91

0   200 m
N
0   0.1 miles

Via Zara

Via San Gallo ✕14

Via Cavour

Via delle Ruote

Via Alfonso Lamarmora

Via Pier Antonio Micheli

Via Venezia

Viale Giacomo Matteotti

Via San Gallo

Via degli Arazzieri

Via Giorgio la Pira

Giardino dei Semplici

Via Gino Capponi

Giardino della Gherardesca

Museo di San Marco 4 ◉

Piazza San Marco

Chiesa della Santissima Annunziata ◉6

Via Giuseppe Giusti

Via Cesare Battisti

◉ Galleria dell'Accademia

Via Cavour

Via Ricasoli

Piazza della SS Annunziata

Via Laura

◉5 Museo degli Innocenti

Via dei Fibbiai

Borgo Pinti

✕15

26 🔒

21 🔒
Pucci

Via dei Servi

20 🛍

25 🔒

Via del Castellaccio

Piazza Brunelleschi

Via degli Alfani

Via della Colonna

19 ✪

Via Nuova de' Caccini

Via Luigi Carlo Farini

Via dei Pilastri

Via Bufalini

Piazza di Santa Maria Nuova

Via della Pergola

Via Sant'Egidio

Borgo Pinti

17 🔒

18 🔒

Via dei Pepi

Via di Mezzo

Via del Proconsolo

Via dell'Oriuolo

23 🔒

Via Fiesolana

Borgo degli Albizi

Via Pietrapiana

Sights

Museo delle Cappelle Medicee

MAUSOLEUM

1 MAP P80, C5

Nowhere is Medici conceit expressed so explicitly as in the Medici Chapels. Adorned with granite, marble, semiprecious stones and some of Michelangelo's most beautiful sculptures, it is the burial place of 49 dynasty members. Francesco I lies in the dark, imposing **Cappella dei Principi** (Chapel of Princes) alongside Ferdinando I and II and Cosimo I, II and III. Lorenzo II Magnifico is buried in the graceful **Sagrestia Nuova** (New Sacristy), which was Michelangelo's first architectural

Michelangelo Essential

For hardcore Michelangelo lovers, no sculptures are more haunting or serenely beautiful than those decorating Medici graves in the sacristy of the Museo delle Cappelle Medicee: *Dawn and Dusk* on the sarcophagus of Lorenzo, Duke of Urbino; *Night and Day* on the sarcophagus of Lorenzo's son Giuliano (note the unfinished face of 'Day' and the youth of the sleeping woman drenched in light aka 'Night'); and *Madonna and Child,* which adorns Lorenzo's tomb.

work. (Medici Chapels; ☎055 064 94 30; www.bargellomusei.beniculturali.it/musei/2/medicee; Piazza Madonna degli Aldobrandini 6; adult/reduced €9/2; ⏰8.15am-2pm, closed 2nd & 4th Sun, 1st, 3rd & 5th Mon of month)

Basilica di San Lorenzo

BASILICA

2 MAP P80, C5

Considered one of Florence's most harmonious examples of Renaissance architecture, this unfinished basilica was the Medici parish church and mausoleum. It was designed by Brunelleschi in 1425 for Cosimo the Elder and built over a 4th-century church. In the solemn interior, look for Brunelleschi's austerely beautiful **Sagrestia Vecchia** (Old Sacristy) with its sculptural decoration by Donatello. Michelangelo was commissioned to design the facade in 1518, but his design in white Carrara marble was never executed, hence the building's rough, unfinished appearance. (☎055 21 40 42; www.operamedicealaurenziana.org; Piazza San Lorenzo; €7, with Biblioteca Medicea Laurenziana €9.50; ⏰10am-5.30pm Mon-Sat)

Biblioteca Medicea Laurenziana

LIBRARY

3 MAP P80, C5

Beyond the Basilica di San Lorenzo ticket office lie peaceful cloisters framing a garden with orange trees. Stairs lead up the loggia to the Biblioteca Medicea Laurenzi-

Biblioteca Medicea Laurenziana

ana, commissioned by Giulio de' Medici (Pope Clement VII) in 1524 to house the extensive Medici library (started by Cosimo the Elder and greatly added to by Lorenzo Il Magnifico). The extraordinary staircase in the vestibule, intended as a 'dark prelude' to the magnificent **Sala di Lettura** (Reading Room), was designed by Michelangelo. (Medici Library; 📞055 293 79 11; www.bml.firenze.sbn.it; Piazza San Lorenzo 9; €3, incl Basilica di San Lorenzo €8.50; ⏱9.30am-1.30pm Mon-Fri)

Museo di San Marco   MUSEUM

4 ◉ MAP P80, E3

At the heart of Florence's university area sits **Chiesa di San Marco** and an adjoining 15th-century Dominican monastery where both gifted painter Fra' Angelico (c 1395–1455) and the sharp-tongued Savonarola piously served God. Today the monastery, aka one of Florence's most spiritually uplifting museums, showcases the work of Fra' Angelico. After centuries of being known as 'Il Beato Angelico' (literally 'The Blessed Angelic One') or simply 'Il Beato' (The Blessed), the Renaissance's most blessed religious painter was made a saint by Pope John Paul II in 1984. (📞055 238 86 08; Piazza San Marco 3; adult/reduced €8/2; ⏱8.15am-1.50pm Mon-Fri, to 4.50pm Sat & Sun, closed 1st, 3rd & 5th Sun, 2nd & 4th Mon of month)

Museo degli Innocenti · MUSEUM

5 ⊙ MAP P80, F4

Shortly after its founding in 1421, Brunelleschi designed the loggia for Florence's **Ospedale degli Innocenti**, a foundling hospital and Europe's first orphanage, built by the wealthy silk-weavers' guild to care for unwanted children. Inside, a highly emotive, state-of-the-art museum explores its history, climaxing with a sensational collection of frescoes and artworks that once decorated the hospital and a stunning rooftop-cafe terrace (fab city views). Brunelleschi's use of rounded arches and Roman capitals marks it as arguably the first building of the Renaissance. (☎055 203 73 08; www.museodegl innocenti.it; Piazza della Santissima Annunziata 13; adult/reduced €7/5; ⊙10am-7pm)

Chiesa della Santissima Annunziata · CHURCH

6 ⊙ MAP P80, F3

Established in 1250 by the founders of the Servite order and rebuilt by Michelozzo and others in the mid-15th century, this Renaissance church is most remarkable for the post-Renaissance painters who worked here together and helped found the mannerist school. There are frescoes by Andrea del Castagno in the first two chapels on the left of the church, and the frescoes in Michelozzo's atrium include work by del Sarto as well as Jacopo Pontormo and Il Rosso Fiorentino (the Redhead from

Fresco detail, Palazzo Meici-Riccardi

Florence). (Piazza della Santissima Annunziata; ⏰ 7.30am-12.30pm & 4-6.30pm)

Palazzo Medici-Riccardi PALACE

7 ◉ MAP P80, D4

Cosimo the Elder entrusted Michelozzo with the design of the family's town house in 1444. The result was this palace, a blueprint that influenced the construction of Florentine family residences such as Palazzo Pitti and Palazzo Strozzi. The upstairs chapel, **Cappella dei Magi**, is covered in wonderfully detailed frescoes (c 1459–63) by Benozzo Gozzoli, a pupil of Fra' Angelico, and is one of the supreme achievements of Renaissance painting. Only 10 visitors are allowed at a time into the Cappella dei Magi. In high season, reserve in advance at the ticket desk. During your visit, take time to spy various Medici family members in Gozzoli's frescoes, whose ostensible theme of Procession of the Magi to Bethlehem is but a slender pretext for portraying members of the Medici clan in their best light; spy Lorenzo il Magnifico and Cosimo the Elder in the crowd. Should you be wondering, the chapel was reconfigured to accommodate a baroque staircase, hence the oddly split fresco. (📞 055 276 03 40; www.palazzomedici.it; Via Cavour 3; adult/reduced €7/4; ⏰ 8.30am-7pm Thu-Tue)

A Green Retreat 🌲

When world-class art and architecture tires, retreat to the **Giardino dei Semplici** (Orto Botanico; Via Pier Antonio Micheli 3; adult/reduced €6/3; ⏰ 10am-7pm Thu-Tue summer, to 4pm Sat & Sun winter) for a peaceful stroll through Florence's botanical gardens, created in 1545 to furnish medicine to the Medici and managed today by the university. Its greenhouse is fragrant with citrus blossoms, and medicinal plants, Tuscan spices, 220 tree types and wildflowers from the Apennines pepper its 2.3 hectares. Don't miss the magnificent yew tree, planted in 1720, and an ornamental cork oak from 1805. Themed footpaths cross the gardens.

Eating

Mercato Centrale FOOD HALL €

8 ✖ MAP P80, C4

Wander the maze of stalls crammed with fresh produce at Florence's oldest and largest food market, on the ground floor of an iron-and-glass structure designed by architect Giuseppe Mengoni in 1874. Head to the 1st floor's buzzing, thoroughly contemporary food hall with dedicated cookery school

Florence's Finest Last Supper

Once part of a sprawling Benedictine monastery, the largely unsung **Cenacolo di Sant'Apollonia** (☑055 238 86 07; www.polomusealetoscana. beniculturali.it; Via XXVII Aprile 1; admission free; ☺8.15am-1.50pm daily, closed 1st, 3rd & 5th Sat & Sun of month) harbours arguably the city's most remarkable Last Supper scene. Painted by Andrea del Castagno in the 1440s, it is one of the first works of its kind to effectively apply Renaissance perspective. It possesses a haunting power with its vivid colours – especially the almost abstract squares of marble painted above the Apostles' heads – as well as the dark, menacing figure of Judas.

and artisan stalls cooking steaks, burgers, tripe *panini,* vegetarian dishes, pizza, gelato, pastries and pasta. (☑055 239 97 98; www. mercatocentrale.it; Piazza del Mercato Centrale 4; dishes €5-15; ☺market 7am-3pm Mon-Fri, to 5pm Sat, food hall 8am-midnight; ☎)

Trattoria Mario   TUSCAN €

9 ✖ MAP P80, D4

Arrive by noon to ensure a spot at this noisy, busy, brilliant trattoria – a legend that retains its soul (and allure with locals) despite being in every guidebook. Charming Fabio, whose grandfather opened the place in 1953, is front of house while big brother Romeo and nephew Francesco cook with speed in the kitchen. No advance reservations; cash only. (☑055 21 85 50; www.trattoria-mario.com; Via Rosina 2r; meals €25; ☺noon-3.30pm Mon-Sat, closed 3 weeks Aug; ❄)

La Ménagère   INTERNATIONAL €€

10 ✖ MAP P80, D4

Be it breakfast, lunch, dinner, coffee or cocktails, this industrial-styled space lures Florence's hip brigade. The concept store is a fashionable one-stop shop for chic china and tableware, designer kitchen gear and fresh flowers. For daytime dining, pick from retro sofas in the boutique, banquette seating or bar stools in the bistro or a table between flower pots in the conservatory-style restaurant. (☑055 075 06 00; www.lamenagere. it; Via de' Ginori 8r; meals €15-70; ☺7am-2am; ☎)

My Sugar   GELATO €

11 ✖ MAP P80, D4

Young artisan ice-cream maker Alberto Bati, partner Giulia and sister Deborah have quickly lured a huge local following with their contemporary artisan *gelateria* near Piazza San Marco. Sensational flavours include dark chocolate with Chianti red wine, black sesame, mint and basil, and black sesame and melacotta (a wonderful fusion of ricotta, honey, cinnamon and apple). Vegan options, frozen yoghurt and milkshakes too. Cash only. (☑ 393 0696042; Via de' Ginori 49r; cones €2.50-4.50, tubs €2.50-5; ⏱ 1-11pm summer, to 8.30pm winter, closed Jan & Feb)

Trattoria Sergio Gozzi

TRATTORIA €

12 ✖ MAP P80, C4

Keep things simple with a traditional Tuscan lunch at this two-room trattoria, tucked between cheap leather shops near Mercato Centrale. Dining is at marble-topped tables in a spartan vintage interior clearly unchanged since 1915 when it opened. Expect all the classics: plenty of pasta, roast meats, tripe and *bollito misto*

Hipster Hang-out

Whatever the time of day, uber-cool concept store and bistro La Ménagère is the hot spot to hobnob with Florentine hipsters; this all-round hybrid is a great breakfast spot too.

(boiled beef, chicken and tongue) included. (☑ 055 28 19 41; Piazza San Lorenzo 8r; meals €25; ⏱ 10am-4pm Mon-Sat)

Da Nerbone

FAST FOOD €

13 ✖ MAP P80, C4

Forge your way past cheese, meat and sausage stalls on the ground floor of the Mercato Centrale (p85)

Da Nerbone

Who's That Bloke?

Name *David*

Occupation World's most famous sculpture.

Vital statistics Height: 516cm tall; weight: 19 tonnes of mediocre-quality pearly white marble from the Fantiscritti quarries in Carrara.

Spirit Young biblical hero in meditative pose who, with the help of God, defeats an enemy more powerful than himself. Scarcely visible sling emphasises victory of innocence and intellect over brute force.

Commissioned In 1501 by the Opera del Duomo for the cathedral, but subsequently placed in front of the Palazzo Vecchio on Piazza della Signoria, where it stayed until 1873.

Famous journeys It took 40 men four days to transport the statue on rails from Michelangelo's workshop behind the cathedral to Piazza della Signoria in 1504. Its journey from here, through the streets of Florence, to its current purpose-built tribune in the Galleria dell'Accademia in 1873, took seven long days.

Outstanding features (a) His expression, which, from the left profile, appears serene, Zen and boylike, and from the right, concentrated, manly and highly charged in anticipation of the gargantuan Goliath he is about to slay; (b) the sense of counterbalanced weight rippling through his body, from the tension in his right hip on which he leans to his taut left arm.

Why the small penis? In classical art a large or even normal-sized packet was not deemed elegant, hence the daintier size.

And the big head and hands? *David* was designed to stand up high on a cathedral buttress in the apse, from where his head and hands would have appeared in perfect proportion.

Beauty treatments Body scrub with hydrochloric acid (1843); clay and cellulose pulp 'mud pack', bath in distilled water (2004).

Occupational hazards Over the centuries he's been struck by lightning, attacked by rioters and had his toes bashed with a hammer. The two pale white lines visible on his lower left arm is where his arm got broken during the 1527 revolt when the Medici were kicked out of Florence. Giorgio Vasari, then a child, picked up the pieces and 16 years later had them sent to Cosimo I who restored the statue, so the story goes.

to join the lunchtime queue at Ner-bone, in the biz since 1872. Go local and order *trippa alla fiorentina* (tripe and tomato stew) or follow the crowd with a feisty *panini con bollito* (a hefty boiled-beef bun, dunked in the meat's juices before serving). Eat standing up or fight for a table.

Forge your way into the market using the Via Sant' Antonino entrance and turn immediately left to find Da Nerbone. (Piazza del Mercato Centrale; meals €5-10; ⊘7am-2pm Mon-Sat)

Antica Trattoria da Tito
TRATTORIA €€

14 ⊗ MAP P80, F1

The 'No well done meat here' sign, strung in the window, says it all: the best of Tuscan culinary tradition is the only thing this iconic trattoria serves. In business since 1913, Da Tito does everything right – tasty Tuscan dishes like onion soup and wild boar pasta, served with friendly gusto and hearty goodwill to a local crowd. Don't be shy to enter. (⊘055 47 24 75; www.trattoriadatito.it; Via San Gallo 112r; meals €30; ⊘noon-3pm & 7-11pm Mon-Sat)

Carabé
GELATO €

15 ⊗ MAP P80, E4

Traditional Sicilian gelato, *granita* (crushed ice made with coffee, fresh fruit or locally grown pistachios and almonds) and brioche (Sicilian ice-cream sandwich);

Fish Friday, Steak Saturday 🍽

In the finest of Tuscan dining tradition, many a trattoria address in Florence cooks up a different traditional dish each day of the week. For the folks at Trattoria Mario (p86), Monday and Thursday are tripe days, Friday is fish and Saturday sees local Florentines flock in for a brilliantly blue *bistecca alla fiorentina* (traditonal Florentine T-bone steak).

handy if you're waiting in line to see *David*. (⊘055 28 94 76; www.parcocarabe.it; Via Ricasoli 60r; tubs & cones €2.50-8.50; ⊘10am-midnight, closed mid-Dec–mid-Jan)

Drinking

PanicAle
COCKTAIL BAR

16 ⊖ MAP P80, C3

Still lovingly known as Lo Sverso (its original name) by many a Florentine socialite, this super-stylish bar is a gem. In a part of town where hipster addresses are scarce, there's no finer spot for an expertly crafted cocktail mixed with homemade syrups (try the basil), craft beer on tap or home-brewed ginger ale. DJs spin tunes many a weekend.

The same Dutch-Italian team is behind the laid-back, equally appealing **De Plek** (⊘348 5903187;

Bakery Break: Pugi 🍽

Should you be queuing to see *David*, **Pugi** (☎055 28 09 81; www.focacceria-pugi.it; Piazza San Marco 9b; per kilogram €15-25; ⏰7.45am-8pm Mon-Sat, closed 2 weeks mid-Aug) is a perfect two-minute hop from the Galleria dell'Accademia. The inevitable line outside the door says it all. The bakery is a Florentine favourite for pizza slices and chunks of *schiacciata* (Tuscan flatbread) baked up plain, spiked with salt and rosemary, or topped or stuffed with whatever delicious edible goodies are in season. Grab a numbered ticket, drool over the sweet and savoury treats demanding to be devoured, and wait for your number to be called.

www.facebook.com/deplekfirenze; Via Panicale 7r; meals €25, brunch €10-12; ⏰11am-midnight Mon-Fri, 5pm-midnight Sat) eatery next door. (☎335 5473530; www.facebook.com/PanicAleFirenze; Via Panicale 7-9r; ⏰5.30pm-1am Mon-Wed & Sun, to 2am Thu-Sat)

Rex Café   BAR

17 🍸 MAP P80, G6

A firm long-term favourite (since 1990), down-to-earth Rex maintains its appeal. Behind the bar Virginia and Lorenzo shake a mean cocktail, using homemade syrups and artisanal spirits like ginger- or carrot-flavoured vodka, pepper rum and laurel vermouth. The artsy, Gaudí-inspired interior is as much art gallery and nightlife stage as simple bar.

DJ sets at weekends and bags of fun events; check its Facebook page (www.facebook.com/rex. firenze) for the week's agenda. (☎055 248 03 31; www.rexfirenze. com; Via Fiesolana 25r; ⏰8pm-3am)

Bitter Bar   COCKTAIL BAR

18 🍸 MAP P80, G6

The 1920s provide the sassy inspiration behind this speakeasy where ordering anything so mundane as a Sex on a Beach is simply not done. Mixologist Cristian Guitti experiments with plenty of unusual bitters, infusions and fresh ingredients to keep cocktail aficionados on their toes, while tasting notes on the tantalising menu – 'sweet smooth', 'fresh and delicate', 'for gin lovers' – pander to the less initiated. (☎340 5499258; www.bitterbarfirenze.it; Via di Mezzo 28r; ⏰9pm-2am Mon-Sat)

Caffè del Verone   CAFE

At home in Ospedale degli Innocenti's *verone* (drying room) where linen at the foundling hospital was hung up to dry in the 15th century, this peaceful rooftop cafe (see 5 ⊙ Map p80, F4) on the 5th floor of the Museo degli Innocenti (p84) is one of San Marco's best-kept secrets. Lounging over drinks on the romantic loggia proffers a magnificent vista of Florentine rooftops and Tuscan hills beyond. (392 4982559; www.facebook.com/CaffedelVeroneRooftopFlorence; Piazza della Santissima Annunziata 13, Museo degli Innocenti; 8.30am-7pm Mon, to 9pm Tue-Sat, 9am-7pm Sun;)

Entertainment

Teatro della Pergola   THEATRE

19 MAP P80, G5

Beautiful city theatre with stunning entrance; host to classical concerts October to April. (055 2 26 41; www.teatrodellapergola.com; Via della Pergola 18)

A Secret Terrace

When the crowds get too much, retreat to the elegant rooftop cafe of the Museo degli Innocenti for an *aperitivo*. There is no finer time to enjoy the sweeping panorama from this 'secret' terrace than at dusk when the sun turns the city pink.

Shopping

Street Doing   VINTAGE

20 MAP P80, F4

Vintage couture for men and women is what this extraordinary rabbit warren of a boutique –

Mercato Centrale (p85)

TUPUNGATO/SHUTTERSTOCK ©

The Medici Family

Nowhere is a family name as linked with a city's identity as in Florence. Harking from the Mugello region north of Florence, the Medici were involved in the wool trade in the 13th and early 14th century. Though successful, they only came to prominence during the late 14th century, when Giovanni di Bicci de' Medici (1360–1429) established the Medici Bank. By the 15th century it was the largest in Europe. Giovanni's son Cosimo ('The Elder'; 1389–1464) used the vast family fortune to control local politics, becoming *gran maestro* (unofficial head of state) of the Florentine republic in 1434. A humanist, he was an enlightened patron of Florentine culture and arts.

Cosimo's son Piero (1416–69) succeeded his father as *gran maestro* but didn't have his penchant for patronage or skill in politics. His son and heir Lorenzo ('The Magnificent'; 1449–92) fully embraced his grandfather's interest in politics and culture, but had no interest in the bank. After his death it became apparent that the bank was in financial trouble, a situation exacerbated by his incompetent son and heir Piero (1472–1503). Piero's short reign as *gran maestro* culminated in the dynasty's exile from Florence in 1494.

Lorenzo's reputation and wealth had ensured that his second son, Giovanni di Lorenzo de' Medici (1475–1521), attained a powerful position in the Church; he became pope in 1513 (as Leo X). His cousin Giulio de' Medici (1478–1535) followed in his footsteps, being elected pope in 1523 and taking the name Clement VII. Both popes continued the Medici tradition of arts patronage. The Medici returned to Florence in 1512, but few were as talented or successful as their forebears. The most impressive was Cosimo I (1519–74), an ambitious soldier who became Duke of Florence and then the first Grand Duke of Tuscany. He was also a great patron of the arts.

After the Medici's defeat by the House of Lorraine, Anna Maria Luisa de' Medici (1667–1743) willed the family's assets (including its magnificent art collection) to the Tuscan state, provided that nothing was ever removed from Florence.

surely the city's largest collection of vintage – is about. Carefully curated garments and accessories are in excellent condition and feature all the top Italian designers: beaded 1950s Gucci clutch bags, floral 1960s Pucci dresses, Valentino shades from every decade. Fashionistas, *this* is heaven. (☎055 538 13 34; www. streetdoingvintage.it; Via dei Servi 88r; ⏱10.30am-7.30pm Mon-Sat, from 2.30pm Sun)

Scriptorium ARTS & CRAFTS

21 🔒 MAP P80, E5

A mooch around this upmarket boutique is worth it, if only to dip into the utterly cinematic courtyard of 16th- to 18th-century Palazzo Pucci in which it's hidden. Scriptorium crafts exquisite leather boxes and books, calligraphy nibs and pens, and old-world wax seals in every colour under the sun. (☎055 238 26 20; www. facebook.com/scriptoriumatelier; Via de' Pucci 4; ⏱10am-1pm & 3.30-7pm Mon-Fri, 10am-1pm Sat)

Penko JEWELLERY

22 🔒 MAP P80, C5

Renaissance jewels and gems inspire the designs of third-generation jeweller Paolo Penko, who works with his son in the atelier his grandfather opened in the 1950s. Everything is handmade, as the mass of vintage tools strewn on the workbench attests. Drop in at the right moment and Paolo can mint you your very own Florentine

San Lorenzo & San Marco Shopping

Scriptorium

JULIET COOMBE/LONELY PLANET ©

florin in bronze, silver or gold. (☎055 21 16 61; www.paolopenko. com; Via Ferdinando Zannetti 14-16r; ◷9.30am-7pm Mon-Sat)

Mrs Macis FASHION & ACCESSORIES

23 🔒 MAP P80, G6

Workshop and showroom of the talented Carla Macis, this eye-catching boutique – dollhouse-like in design – specialises in very feminine 1950s, '60s and '70s clothes and jewellery made from new and recycled fabrics. Every piece is unique and fabulous. (☎055 247 67 00; www.facebook.com/mrsmacis; Borgo Pinti 38r; ◷4-7.30pm Mon, 10am-1.30pm & 4-7.30pm Tue-Sat)

Midinette FASHION & ACCESSORIES

24 🔒 MAP P80, B4

From the shabby-chic floor – partly original tiles, partly bare paint – to the retro-inspired fashion, this clothing and accessory boutique for women is impossibly romantic and creative. Florentine designer Filomena Gullo sources her fabrics in Tuscany and every garment proudly brandishes a 'Made in Italy' label. (☎055 088 16 56; www.facebook.com/pg/midi nettefirenze; Piazza della Stazione 51r; ◷10.30am-8pm Mon-Sat, from 11am Sun)

Eataly

Bartolini HOMEWARES

25 🔒 MAP P80, E5

Foodies with even the mildest interest in cooking will find Florence's most famous kitchen shop absolutely fascinating. Don't miss the collection of pasta-making tools. (📞055 29 14 97; www.dino bartolini.it; Via dei Servi 72r; ⏰10am-7pm Mon-Sat)

Scarpelli Mosaici ART

26 🔒 MAP P80, E4

The entire Scarpelli family works hard to preserve the art of *pietre dure*, puzzle-like marble mosaics, at this lovely boutique and workshop tucked beneath a red-brick vaulted ceiling. If staff have time, they'll give you a quick introduction to this beautiful, yet incredibly painstaking, craft. (📞055 21 25 87; www.scarpellimosaici.it; Via Ricasoli 59r; ⏰9.30am-6.30pm Mon-Fri, to 1pm Sat)

One-Stop Shop 🍴

Epicureans, follow Florence's foodie crowd to **Eataly** (📞055 015 36 01; www.eataly.net; Via de' Martelli 22r; ⏰10am-10.30pm; 📶), a one-stop culinary shop for everything Tuscan. Peruse beautifully arranged aisles laden with olive oils, conserved vegetables, pasta, rice, biscuits and so on. There are fresh bakery and deli counters, fridges laden with seemingly every cheese under the Italian sun, and a coffee bar with outdoor seating. Many products are local and/or organic; most are by small producers. Upstairs is a wine cellar with 600 labels, a cooking school, summer terrace and the epicurean Osteria di Sopra serving lunch and dinner.

Walking Tour 🚶

A Day in Fiesole

Set in cypress-studded hills 9km northeast of Florence, this bijou hilltop village has seduced visitors for centuries with its cool breezes, olive groves, Renaissance-styled villas and spectacular views. Before you arrive, download the map from the website of Fiesole's tourist office (www.fiesoleforyou.it). It shows three walking routes through the village, as well as tips for discovering the most breathtaking views of Florence.

Walk Facts

Start Piazza Mino da Fiesole

Finish Piazza Mino da Fiesole

Length 1km; one hour (plus 20 minutes by bus from/to Florence)

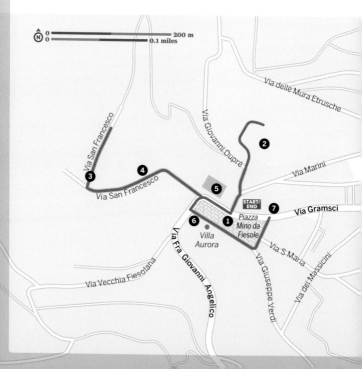

❶ Piazza People-Watching

Transport hub, *passeggiata* hot spot and host to an antiques market on the first Sunday of each month, **Piazza Mino da Fiesole** is the village heart. Claim a stone bench or sit on a cafe terrace and watch the action unfold.

❷ Etruscan Ruins

Explore the **Area Archeologica** (☎055 596 12 93; www.museidifiesole. it; Via Portigiani 1; adult/reduced €7/5, with Archaeological Museum €10/6; ⏰9am-7pm summer, shorter hours winter), a pretty site with ruins of an Etruscan temple (Fiesole was founded in the 7th century BC by the Etruscans), Roman baths, an archaeological museum with exhibits from the Bronze Age to the Roman period, and a 1st-century-BC Roman theatre where live music and theatre fill summer evenings during the **Estate Fiesolana** (June to August).

❸ Chiesa e Convento di San Francesco

Hike up steep, walled, pedestrian **Via San Francesco** and be blown away by the staggeringly beautiful panorama of Florence that unfolds from the terrace adjoining this 15th-century **church** (⏰9am-noon & 3-6pm) and former convent at the top.

❹ Lunch with View

Feast on hypnotic views and delicious Tuscan cuisine on the panoramic terrace of **La Reggia degli Etruschi** (☎055 5 93 85; www.lareggiadeglietruschi.com; Via San Francesco; meals €30; ⏰7-9.30pm Mon-Wed, 12.30-1.30pm & 7-9.30pm Thu-Sun), halfway down the hill.

❺ Cattedrale di San Romolo

Continue down the hill and seek some cool air in Fiesole's **cathedral** (Piazza Mino da Fiesole; admission free; ⏰7.30am-noon & 3-5pm), begun in the 11th century. A glazed terracotta statue of San Romolo by Giovanni della Robbia guards the entrance inside.

❻ An Afternoon Drink

Enjoy an *aperitivo* at **JJ Hill** (☎055 5 93 24; Piazza Mino da Fiesole 40; ⏰6pm-2.30am summer, shorter hours winter), an Irish pub with a tip-top beer list. Or lounge on the more refined, pagoda-covered terrace of **Villa Aurora** (☎055 5 93 63; www. villaurorafiesole.com; Piazza Mino da Fiesole 39; meals €30; ⏰noon-2.30pm & 7-10.30pm), a favourite for its romantic Florence view since 1860.

❼ A Sunset Bike Ride

Fire up the romantic in you with a 2½-hour, 21km guided bike ride (€50 including bike hire) by sunset back to Florence with **FiesoleBike** (☎345 3350926; www.fiesolebike.it), a creative bike rental/guiding outfit run with passion by local Fiesole lad Giovanni Crescioli (a qualified biking and hiking guide to boot). His 'sunset' tour departs daily from Piazza Mino da Fiesole at 5pm in season; book in advance online.

Explore ◈

Santa Croce

Despite being only a hop, skip and jump from the city's major museums, this ancient part of Florence is far removed from the tourist maelstrom. The streets behind the basilica are home to plenty of locals, all of whom seem to be taking their neighbourhood's reinvention as hipster central – epicentre of the city's bar and club scene – with remarkable aplomb.

The Short List

○ **Museo del Bargello (p102)** *Discovering plenty more Davids and unsung Michelangelos in Florence's finest sculpture museum.*

○ **Il Teatro del Sale (p105)** *Tucking into hearty Tuscan fare over live theatre courtesy of Florence's original rebel chef.*

○ **Basilica di Santa Croce (p100)** *Dipping into frescoed chapels and uncovering the graves of greats in this awe-inspiring barn of a Franciscan basilica.*

○ **Terrazza Menoni (p111)** *Joining locals in the amicable bun fight for the best seasonal produce at Mercato di Sant'Ambrogio followed by lunch at this 1920s butcher's stall.*

○ **Ditta Artigianale (p112)** *Sipping craft coffee and cocktails with Florentine A-listers.*

Getting There

🚶 From Piazza della Stazione walk southeast via Via de' Panzani, Via de' Cerretani and Via del Proconsolo to Museo del Bargello. Take Via Ghibellina and turn right at Via Giuseppe Verdi to Piazza di Santa Croce.

Santa Croce Map on p106

Basilica di Santa Croce (p100) ROMAN SIGAEV/SHUTTERSTOCK ©

Top Experience 📷
Wonder at the
Basilica di Santa Croce

The austere interior of this massive Franciscan basilica is a surprise when compared with its magnificent neo-Gothic facade, which is enlivened by varying shades of coloured marble. Though most visitors come to see the tombs of Michelangelo, Dante, Galileo and Machiavelli in the nave, it's the Giotto chapel frescoes that are the real highlights.

◉ MAP P106, C3

☎ 055 246 61 05

www.santacroceopera.it

Piazza di Santa Croce 16

adult/reduced €8/6

🕑 9.30am-5.30pm Mon-Sat, from 2pm Sun

Frescoed Chapels

Giotto's murals feature John the Baptist in the **Cappella Peruzzi** (1310–20), while the **Cappella Bardi** (1320-28) features scenes from the life of St Francis. Giotto's assistant and loyal pupil, Taddeo Gaddi, frescoed **Cappella Maggiore** and **Cappella Baroncelli** (1328–38).

Sagrestia

From the transept chapels, a doorway designed by Michelozzo leads into a corridor, off which is the enchanting 14th-century Sacristy with Taddeo Gaddi's fresco of the Crucifixion. The large painted wooden cross (c 1288) by Cimabue was one of many artworks to be damaged in the 1966 floods which inundated Santa Croce in more than 4m of water.

Cappella de' Pazzi

Backtrack to the church and follow the 'Uscita' (exit) sign, opposite the main entrance, to access the basilica's two serene cloisters designed by Brunelleschi. His unfinished Cappella de' Pazzi is notable for its harmonious lines and restrained terracotta medallions of the Apostles by Luca della Robbia, and is a masterpiece of Renaissance architecture.

Cenacolo

Continue to the second cloister. Inside the cavernous Refectory, Taddeo Gaddi's dazzling *The Last Supper* (1334–56) fills the entire far wall, but it's Georgio Vasari's *The Last Supper* (1546) that steals the show. Submerged in floodwater for at least 12 hours, the severely damaged oil painting was returned to Santa Croce following 50 years of restoration in 2016.

★ Top Tips

o Walk through the church bookshop to access the **Scuola del Cuoio**, a traditional leather school where you can see bags being fashioned and buy the finished products.

o In 1817 the French writer Stendhal experienced a racing heartbeat, nausea and dizziness when exiting the basilica. His reaction to its cultural richness (and that of Florence as a whole) has been shared by many other visitors, hence the description 'Stendhal Syndrome'. Consider yourself warned.

✕ Take a Break

Join locals for a quick tasty trattoria lunch at Il Giova (p109).

For an *aperitivo*, head to one of the many bars on Via de' Benci.

Top Experience 📷
Learn about Michelangelo at the Museo del Bargello

It was from fortresslike Palazzo del Bargello that the podestà (governing magistrate) meted out justice until 1502. Today the building safeguards Italy's most comprehensive collection of Tuscan Renaissance sculpture, including Michelangelo's best early works. While crowds clamour to see his David, few rush here – rendering the Bargello a highly rewarding experience.

◉ MAP P106, A2

☎ 055 238 86 06

www.bargellomusei.
beniculturali.it

Via del Proconsolo 4

adult/reduced €8/4

🕓 8.15am-2pm, closed
2nd & 4th Sun, 1st, 3rd &
5th Mon of month

Michelangelo

Michelangelo was just 21 when he created the drunken, grape-adorned *Bacchus* (1496–97) displayed in the ground-floor **Sala di Michelangelo e della Scultura del Cinque Cento** (first door on the right after entering the interior courtyard from the ticket office). Other Michelangelo works include the marble bust of *Brutus* (c 1539–40), the *David/Apollo* (1530–32) and the large, uncompleted roundel of the *Madonna and Child with the Infant St John* (1503–05; aka the *Tondo Pitti*).

Salone di Donatello

The majestic salon where the city's general council met now showcases works by Donatello and other 15th-century sculptors. Don't miss his *St George* (1416–17), originally on the facade of Chiesa di Orsanmichele and now within a tabernacle at the hall's far end, which brought a new sense of perspective and movement to Italian sculpture.

Yet it is Donatello's two versions of *David*, a favourite subject for sculptors, that really fascinate: Donatello fashioned his slender, youthful dressed image in marble in 1408 and his fabled bronze between 1439 and 1443. The latter is extraordinary – the more so when you consider it was the first freestanding naked statue to be sculpted since classical times.

The Della Robbias

The 2nd floor moves into the 16th century with a superb collection of terracotta pieces by the prolific della Robbia family, including Andrea's *Ritratto idealizia di fanciullo* (Bust of a Boy; c 1475) and Giovanni's *Pietà* (1514). Instantly recognisable, Giovanni's works are more flamboyant than those of his father Luca or cousin Andrea, using a larger palette of colours.

★ Top Tips

○ Don't try to visit the Bargello and Uffizi together – their collections are too large and important to cram into a single day.

○ Michelangelo devotees can follow a chronological trail of his sculptural works in Florence by visiting *David* at the Galleria dell'Accademia, stopping at the Museo delle Cappelle Medicee to view the sculptures in the Sagrestia Nuova and then heading to the Bargello to admire his second *David* (aka Apollo) and the *Tondo Pitti*. End with family home Casa Buonarroti.

✕ Take a Break

Continue the arty theme with a coffee break, light lunch or afternoon tea at hipster cafe-bookshop Brac (p108).

Grab a quick *panino* or linger over a traditional Tuscan meal at Antico Noè (p110).

Walking Tour

A Night Out in Santa Croce

In this heavily touristed city, it can be hard to find authentic pockets of local life. Fortunately, the fact that the basilica is the only top-drawer sight in Santa Croce means the neighbourhood is blessedly bereft of sightseers – locals flock here to shop, eat, drink and party with their fellow Florentines as a result.

Walk Facts

Start Ponte alle Grazie

Finish Plaza Hotel Lucchesi

Length 2.5km; 45 minutes

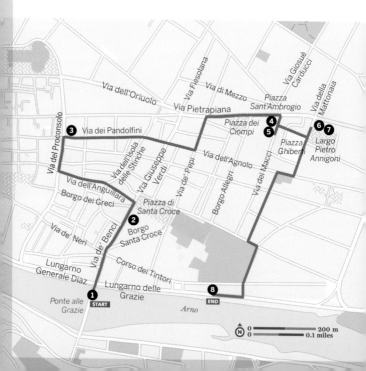

❶ Riverside Lounging

Begin the night out the Florentine way – soaking up the light, view and mood from a bridge across the Arno. Lounge with locals on **Ponte alle Grazie** as the sun softens.

❷ Shopping at Dusk

Dive into trendy Via de' Benci with its bevy of bars and boutiques. Pop into **Boutique Nadine** (☏ 055 247 82 74; www.boutiquenadine.com; Via de' Benci 32r; ☽10.30am-7.30pm Mon-Sat, from 2pm Sun) to browse its vintage clothing, jewellery, homewares and pretty little trinkets displayed in antique cabinets. Continue to the chic fashion boutiques of **Via del Proconsolo**.

❸ Fishing Lab

End your shopping spree with an *aperitivo* with fried anchovies, tuna buns and other fishy nibbles at **Fishing Lab** (☏ 055 24 06 18; www.fishinglab.it; Via del Proconsolo 16r; meals €40; ☽11am-midnight). Peek upstairs at the fragments of 14th- and 15th-century frescoes decorating the enchanting dining room.

❹ Post-Midnight Party

Check out the post-midnight party at **Caffè Sant'Ambrogio** (☏ 055 247 72 77; Piazza Sant'Ambrogio 7r; ☽10am-3am; 🛜). Trendy 30-something Florentines flock here for after-work cocktails, late-night drinks and parties til dawn.

❺ Il Teatro del Sale

Chef Fabio Picchi's **Il Teatro del Sale** (☏ 055 200 14 92; www.teatrodelsale.com; Via dei Macci 111r; brunch/dinner €20/30; ☽noon-2.30pm & 7-11pm Tue-Fri, noon-3pm & 7-11pm Sat, noon-3pm Sun, closed Aug) is an unforgettable experience. Dinner is a hectic, mesmerising symphony of outstanding Tuscan dishes, culminating at 9.30pm in a live performance of drama, music or comedy.

❻ Monkey Bar

Duck into **Monkey Bar** (☏ 055 24 28 62; www.facebook.com/Monkey BarFirenze; Via della Mattonaia 20r; ☽6pm-2am), a noisy pub packed with Florentine and foreign students downing shots, Spritz and well-made Bloody Marys.

❼ Late-Night Drinks

Plunge into the star-lit night and follow the hip crowd to **Largo Pietro Annigoni**. This car-free plaza buzzes with life on summer nights when its alfresco terraces, including **Drogheria** (☏ 055 247 88 69; www.facebook.com/drogheriafire nze; ☽10am-2am), overflow with late-night drinkers.

❽ Hobnob under the Stars

Sip craft cocktails at **Empireo** (☏ 055 262 35 00; www.hotelplazaluc chesi.it; Lungarno della Zecca Vecchia 38; ☽7.30am-midnight; 🛜), one of Florence's most fashionable rooftop bars atop the riverside Plaza Hotel Lucchesi. Views of the Arno and starlit night sky are bewitching. Reserve a table in advance, dress hip to get in, and watch for cocktail masterclasses.

Santa Croce

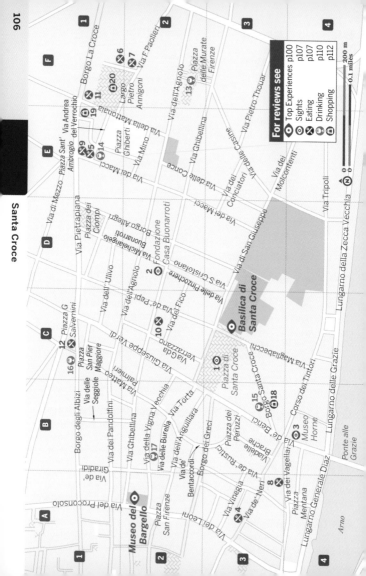

A1 Museo del Bargello

B Via del Proconsolo

F1 Borgo La Croce

Via Andrea del Verrocchio

E Piazza Sant' Ambrogio

Via Sant'

Via dei Macci

Via della Mattonaia

Largo Pietro Annigoni

Via F Paolieri

Piazza delle Murate Firenze

20

6
7
11
19
5
14

9

Piazza Ghiberti

Via Mino

Via dell'Agnolo

13

Via dell'Agnolo

Via Ghibellina

Via delle Conce

Via Pietra Thouar

Via dei Macci

Via dei Conciatori

Via delle Casine

Via dei Molcontenti

Via Tripoli

Via di Mezzo

Via Pietrapiana

Piazza dei Ciompi

Borgo Allegri

Via Michelangelo Buonarroti

Fondazione Casa Buonarroti

Via delle Pinacbere

Via de' Pepi

Via S Cristofano

Via di San Giuseppe

Via dei Macci

Via dell'Ulivo

Via dell'Agnolo

Via del Fico

2

10

Via Ga Verrazzano

Via Giuseppe Verdi

Basilica di Santa Croce

Piazza di Santa Croce

Via Magliabecchi

Piazza G Salvemini

Via Matteo Palmieri

Via delle Seggiole

Via dei Pandolfini

Piazza San Pier Maggiore

Borgo degli Albizi

12

16

Via Ghibellina

Via della Vigna Vecchia

Via delle Burella

Via Torta

Via dell'Anguillara

Borgo dei Greci

Via de' Rustici

Corso dei Tintori

Lungarno della Zecca Vecchia

Museo Horne

3

15

18

1

Via de' Benci

Via de' Bentaccordi

Piazza dei Peruzzi

Via delle Brache

17

Via de' Giraldi

Via Vinegia

Piazza San Firenze

Via dei Leoni

Via de' Neri

4

8

Via de' Vagellai

Piazza Mentana

Lungarno Generale Diaz

Ponte alle Grazie

Lungarno delle Grazie

Arno

For reviews see

●	Top Experiences	p100
◉	Sights	p107
✪	Eating	p107
✪	Drinking	p110
ⓜ	Shopping	p112

0   200 m
0   0.1 miles

Sights

Piazza di Santa Croce   PIAZZA

1 🔘 MAP P106, C3

This square was cleared in the Middle Ages to allow the faithful to gather when the church itself was full. In Savonarola's day, heretics were executed here. Such an open space inevitably found other uses, and from the 14th century it was often the colourful scene of jousts, festivals and *calcio storico* (historic football) matches. The city's 2nd-century amphitheatre took up the area facing the square's western end: Piazza dei Peruzzi, Via de' Bentaccordi and Via Torta mark the oval outline of its course.

Fondazione Casa Buonarroti   MUSEUM

2 🔘 MAP P106, D2

Though Michelangelo never lived in Casa Buonarroti, his heirs devoted some of the artist's hard-earned wealth to the construction of this 17th-century *palazzo* (mansion) to honour his memory. The little museum contains frescoes of the artist's life and two of his most important early works – the serene, bas-relief *Madonna of the Stairs* and the unfinished *Battle of the Centaurs*. (📞055 24 17 52; www.casabuonarroti.it; Via Ghibellina 70; adult/reduced €8/5; ⏰10am-5pm Wed-Mon summer, to 4.30pm winter)

Museo Horne   MUSEUM

3 🔘 MAP P106, B4

One of the many eccentric Brits who made Florence home in the early 20th century, Herbert Percy Horne bought and renovated this Renaissance *palazzo*, then installed his eclectic collection of 14th- and 15th-century Italian art, ceramics, furniture and other oddments. There are a few works by masters such as Giotto and Fra' Filippo Lippi. More interesting is the furniture, some of which is exquisite. (📞055 24 46 61; www.museohorne.it; Via de' Benci 6; adult/reduced €7/5; ⏰10am-2pm Thu-Tue)

Eating

All'Antico Vinaio   OSTERIA €

4 ✖️ MAP P106, A3

The crowd spills out the door of this noisy Florentine thoroughbred, pride and joy of the Mazzanti family since 1991. Push your way to the tables at the back to taste cheese and salami in situ (reservations recommended). Or join the queue at the deli counter for a well-stuffed focaccia wrapped in waxed paper to take away – the quality is outstanding. Pour yourself a glass of wine while you wait. (📞349 3719947, 055 238 27 23; www.allanticovinaio.com; Via de' Neri 65r; tasting platters €10-30; ⏰10am-4pm & 6-11pm Tue-Sat, noon-3.30pm Sun)

Trattoria Cibrèo
TUSCAN €€

5 🍴 MAP P106, E1

Dine at chez Fabio Picchi and you'll instantly understand why a queue gathers outside before it opens. Once inside, revel in top-notch Tuscan cuisine: perhaps *pappa al pomodoro* (a thick soupy mash of tomato, bread and basil) followed by *polpettine di pollo e ricotta* (chicken and ricotta meatballs). No reservations, no credit cards, no pasta and arrive early. (www.cibreo.com; Via dei Macci 122r; meals €30-35; ⏲12.50-2.30pm & 6.50-11pm, closed Aug)

Santarpia
PIZZA €

6 🍴 MAP P106, F1

Florentines can't get enough of the thin-crust Neapolitan pizzas oven-

Pappa al pomodoro

DENIO109/SHUTTERSTOCK ©

fired by master *pizzaiolo* (pizza chef) Giovanni Santarpia at his thoroughly contemporary pizzeria across the road from Mercato di Sant'Ambrogio. Grab a table between brightly spangled walls and open the feast with deep-fried *baccalà* (salted cod), porcini mushrooms or other *fritto* – there is even *pizza fritta con lampre-dotto* (deep-fried pizza with tripe). (📞055 24 58 29; www.santarpia.biz; Largo Pietro Annigoni 9c; pizza €8.50-15; ⏲7.30pm-midnight Tue-Sun; 🛜)

Vivo
SEAFOOD €€

7 🍴 MAP P106, F2

Raw fish, shellfish, oysters and other fishy dishes – all caught in waters around Italy by the Manno family's 30-strong fleet of fishing boats – are cooked up by chef Anna Maria at this fish restaurant, inside a hangar-styled contemporary space with a fishing-boat-shaped bar. Everything is ultra-fresh and the daily changing menu includes many a rare or forgotten fish. (📞333 1824183; www.ristorantevivo.it; Largo Pietro Annigoni 9a/b; seafood platters €15-50, meals €45; ⏲12.30-2.30pm & 7.30-11pm Tue-Sun; 🛜)

Brac
VEGETARIAN €

8 🍴 MAP P106, A3

This hipster cafe-bookshop – a hybrid dining-*aperitivo* address – cooks up inventive, home-style and strictly vegetarian and/or vegan cuisine. Its decor is recycled vintage with the occasional kid's drawing thrown in for that intimate homey touch; the vibe is artsy. Lunchtime ushers in a fantastic-value *piatto unico* (€15) comprising your choice of three dishes served on a single plate. (☏055 094 48 77; www.libreriabrac.net; Via dei Vagellai 18r; meals €20; ☺noon-midnight, closed 2 weeks mid-Aug; 🛜🖊)

Trippaio Sergio Pollini
FAST FOOD €

9 🍴 MAP P106, E1

For a fast munch-on-the-move follow Florentines to this *trippaio* (mobile tripe stand) for a tripe *panino*. Think cow's stomach chopped up, boiled, sliced, bunged between bread and doused in *salsa verde* (pea-green sauce of smashed parsley, garlic, capers and anchovies). A bastion of good old-fashioned Florentine tradition, this *trippaio* is one of the city's busiest. (Piazza Sant' Ambrogio; tripe €3.50; ☺9.30am-3.30pm Mon-Sat)

Enoteca Pinchiorri
TUSCAN €€€

10 🍴 MAP P106, C2

Niçoise chef Annie Féolde applies French techniques to her refined Tuscan cuisine and does it so well that this is the only restaurant in Tuscany to brandish three shiny Michelin stars. Imagine pigeon roasted in a cocoa-bean crust, with a salted-peanut emulsion and black-truffle sauce. The setting is a 16th-century *palazzo* hotel and the wine list is out of this world.

An Afternoon Gelato ❄

Florentines take their gelato seriously and there's healthy rivalry among the operators of local *gelaterie artigianale* (shops selling handmade gelato), who strive to create the city's creamiest, most flavourful and freshest ice cream using seasonal flavours. In Santa Croce, **Vivoli** (☏055 29 23 34; www.vivoli.it; Via dell'Isola delle Stinche 7; tubs €2-10; ☺7.30am-midnight Tue-Sat, from 9am Sun, to 9pm winter) is the gelateria with the greatest number of devotees – try pistachio, pear and caramel or chocolate with orange to understand why. Pay at the cash desk then trade your receipt for the good stuff. No cones, only tubs, plus – unusually for a gelateria – coffee, cakes and comfy inside seating too.

Dress code for gents: preferably a jacket, and most definitely not shorts and/or a short-sleeved shirt, T-shirt or sweater. (☏055 2 63 11; www.enotecapinchiorri.com; Via Ghibellina 87r; 7-/8-course menu €250/275; ☺7.30-10pm Tue-Sat, closed Aug)

Il Giova
TRATTORIA €

11 🍴 MAP P106, F1

Pocket-sized and packed, this cheery trattoria with marigold walls and colourful ceramic-tiled tables is everything a traditional Florentine eating place should be. Dig into century-old dishes like *zuppa della nonna* (grandma's soup), *risotto del giorno* (risotto of the day) or *mafalde al ragù* (long-ribboned pasta with meat sauce) and pride yourself on having found the locals' lunchtime canteen. (055 248 06 39; www.facebook.com/ilGiovafirenze; Borgo La Croce 73r; meals €15; 12.30-3pm & 7.30-11pm Mon-Sat)

Riverside Street Food

'Bringing the countryside to the city' is the driver behind **La Toraia** (www.latoraia.com; Lungarno del Tempio 3450; meals €5-10; noon-midnight mid-Apr–mid-Oct), a cherry-red artisan food truck whose name translates as 'breeding shed'. Parked riverside, a 15-minute stroll east of Piazza di Santa Croce, the truck cooks up sweet 140g burgers, crafted from tender Chianina meat sourced at the family farm in Val di Chiana and topped with melted *pecorino* (sheep's milk cheese).

Real McCoy homemade fries (€4; made from organic Tuscan potatoes grown on the farm, of course), craft beers (€4) from the same valley, and a bunch of tables, chairs and comfy loungers by the river cap off the bucolic alfresco experience.

Antico Noè
OSTERIA €€

12 MAP P106, C1

Don't be put off by the dank alley in which you'll find this old butcher's shop with marble-clad walls, wrought-iron meat hooks and a name inspired by an old Italian vermouth. The drunks loitering outside are generally harmless and the down-to-earth Tuscan fodder served is a real joy. (055 234 08 38; www.anticonoe.com; Volta di San Piero 6-8r; meals €40; noon-2am Mon & Wed-Sat)

Drinking

Le Murate
CAFE

13 MAP P106, F2

This arty cafe-bar in Florence's former jail is where literati meet to talk, create and perform over coffee, drinks and light meals. The literary cafe hosts everything from readings and interviews with authors – Florentine, Italian and international – to film screenings, debates, live music and art exhibitions. Tables are built from recycled window frames and in summer everything spills outside into the brick courtyard. (Caffè Letterario Firenze; 055 234 68 72; www.lemurate.it; Piazza delle Murate; 10.30am-1am Mon-Fri, from 4pm Sat & Sun;)

Caffè Cibrèo
CAFE

14 MAP P106, E1

The cafe arm of Florentine superstar chef Fabio Picci (run by his son Giulio, no less), this charming old-world cafe behind Mercato di Sant'Ambrogio is a quintessential Florentine spot for a mid-morning coffee and sugar-dusted *ciambella* (doughnut ring). (☎055 234 58 53; Via Andrea del Verrocchio 5; ⏱9am-1am, closed Aug)

Quelo COCKTAIL BAR

15 🚍 MAP P106, B3

Hidden down a rather dark and dank street near Basilica di Santa Croce, this tiny food and cocktail bar is a sweet spot for a quick drink between sights or a dusk-time *aperitivo* with generous buffet spread. Check its Facebook page for upcoming DJ sets, live music and other cultural happenings. Interior design is 1950s vintage. (☎055 1999 1474; www.facebook.com/quelobar.firenze; Borgo Santa Croce 15r; ⏱8.30am-2am Mon-Fri, from 6.30pm Sat; 🛜)

Lion's Fountain IRISH PUB

16 🚍 MAP P106, C1

If you have the urge to hear more English than Italian – or to hear local bands play for that matter – this is the place. On a pretty pedestrian square, Florence's busiest Irish pub buzzes in summer when the beer-loving crowd spills across most of the square. Live music and a canary-yellow food 'truck' in the alley around the corner, serving burgers, tacos and chicken wings. (☎055 234 44 12; www.thelionsfountain.com; Borgo degli Albizi 34r; ⏱10am-3am)

Lunch at the Market 🍽

Florentines swear by **Semel** (Piazza Ghiberti 44r; panini €3.50-5; ⏱11.30am-2.30pm Mon-Sat), a pocket-sized sandwich bar with no fixed menu, rather a choice of six gourmet combos, crafted with love by passionate owner and *panini* king Marco Paparozzi. Wash it down with a glass of water or wine, and pride yourself on snagging one of the cheapest, tastiest lunches in town.

For *dolci* (dessert), nip across the street to buy some local, seasonal fruit at the **Mercato di Sant'Ambrogio** (Piazza Ghiberti; ⏱7am-2pm Mon-Sat), the neighbourhood's bustling outdoor food market with an intimate, local flavour. The best day is Saturday when farmers from the region travel here to sell their produce. You can also grab lunch here, at **Terrazza Menoni** (☎055 248 07 78; www.terrazzamenoni.it; Piazza Ghiberti 11; meals €15-20; ⏱noon-2.30pm Mon-Sat).

Full Up CLUB

17 🚍 MAP P106, B2

A variety of sounds energises the crowd at this popular Florentine nightclub, in the biz since 1958, where 20-somethings dance until dawn. (☎055 29 30 06; www.fullupclub.com; Via della Vigna Vecchia 21r; ⏱11pm-4am Thu-Sat Sep-Jun)

Third-Wave Coffee & Gin

With industrial decor and a welcoming, laid-back vibe, **Ditta Artigianale** (☏055 274 15 41; www.dittaartigianale. it; Via de' Neri 32r; ⏱8am-10pm Mon-Thu, to midnight Fri, 9am-midnight Sat, to 11pm Sun; 🛜) – an ingenious coffee roastery and gin bar – is a perfect place to hang any time of day. The creation of three-times Italian barista champion Francesco Sanapo, it's famed for its first-class coffee and outstanding gin cocktails. If you're yearning for a flat white, cold brew tonic or cappuccino made with almond, soy or coconut milk, come here.

Fantastic food is served all day, kicking off with Greek yo-ghurt and muesli, French toast and pancake breakfasts from 9am and culminating with tasty tapas from 7pm when a gourmet *aperitivo* kicks in. Should expertly crafted gin cocktails be your sin, there is no finer address.

Shopping

Aquaflor

COSMETICS

18 🔒 MAP P106, B3

This elegant Santa Croce per-fumery in a vaulted 15th-century *palazzo* exudes romance and exoticism. Artisanal scents are crafted here with tremendous care and precision by master perfumer Sileno Cheloni, who works with precious essences from all over the world, including Florentine iris. Organic soaps, cosmetics and body-care products make equally lovely gifts to take back home.

Should you dream of creating your very own special perfume, count around €1500 for a three-hour bespoke workshop. (☏055 234 34 71; www.aquaflorexperience. com; Borgo Santa Croce 6; ⏱10am-1pm & 2-7pm)

Alla Sosta dei Papi

FOOD & DRINKS

19 🔒 MAP P106, E1

This tiny *enoteca* is a wine-buff one-stop shop. Tuscan wines range from as cheap as chips (bring your own bottle and fill it up for €3.40 per litre) to the very best. Even better, taste before you buy over a glass in the company of cheese and salami platters, crostini and other mouthwatering wine-bar-style nibbles. (☏055 234 11 74; www.sostadeipapi.it; Borgo La Croce 81r; ⏱9am-1.30pm & 4-10pm Tue-Sat)

Mercato delle Pulci

ANTIQUES

20 🔒 MAP P106, F1

Historically at home (alongside the city's fish market) on Piazza dei Ciompi since 1900, Florence's antiques and flea market can now be found opposite Santa Croce's Mercato di Sant'Ambrogio. Peruse its racing-green stalls for a piece of Old Tuscany to take home.

On the last Sunday of each month stalls spill along surrounding streets to form a huge bonanza market, well worth the meander. (Flea Market; Largo Pietro Annigoni; ⏲9am-7.30pm)

Florentine Cuisine 🍽

Be it by sinking your teeth into a flavoursome *bistecca alla fiorentina* (T-bone steak), savouring the taste and aroma of freshly shaved white truffles or sampling rustic specialities such as *trippa alla fiorentina* (tripe slow-cooked with onion, carrot, celery and tomatoes), you're sure to discover plenty of taste sensations when eating in Florence.

Florentine cuisine has stayed faithful to its humble regional roots, relying on fresh local produce and eschewing fussy execution. That's not to say that it lacks refinement – Florence is home to many highly skilled and internationally lauded chefs – but it's true to say that the hallmark of the local cuisine is its simplicity.

When here, be sure to try a *bistecca alla fiorentina,* but be prepared for it to come to the table *al sangue* (bloody). Accompanied by slow-cooked white beans, or sometimes roast potatoes, this signature dish relies on the quality of its Chianina beef (from the Val di Chiana south of Florence) and the skill with which it has been butchered and grilled. Wash it down with a Tuscan red wine – a Chianti Classico, Brunello di Montepulciano or perhaps even a Vino Nobile di Montepulciano.

Other local specialities include *cinghiale* (wild boar), best savoured in autumnal stews; antipasti plates featuring fresh *pecorino* cheese made from sheep's milk, locally cured meats and crostini (lightly toasted pieces of bread topped with liver pâté); and *minestre* (soups) including *zuppa di fagioli* (bean soup), *ribollita* (a 'reboiled' bean, vegetable and bread soup with black cabbage) and *pappa al pomodoro* (a thick bread and tomato soup).

Adventurous eaters need go no further than the city's *trippai* (tripe carts), where tripe *panini* are doused in *salsa verde* (a tasty pea-green sauce of smashed parsley, garlic, capers and anchovies). Such rustic, powerfully flavoured treats stand in stark contrast to the refined joy of white truffles from San Miniato near Pisa – best shaved over a bowl of pasta or risotto – and porcini mushrooms gathered in local forests and tossed through *taglierini* (thin ribbon pasta). Both of these indulgences are surprisingly affordable and utterly delectable.

Explore ⚜

Boboli & San Miniato al Monte

If you start to suffer museum overload (a common occurrence in this culturally resplendent city), you may decide that to stretch your legs and see some sky. If so, the tier of palaces, villas and gardens ascending to the Basilica di San Miniato al Monte, one of the city's oldest and most beautiful churches, will fit the bill perfectly.

The Short List

○ **Giardino di Boboli (p118)** Taking time out in the city's most palatial, fountain- and flower-strewn gardens.

○ **Palazzo Pitti (p116)** Spending a morning devouring art, craft and fashion museums inside this magnificent Medici palace.

○ **La Leggenda dei Frati (p124)** Lunching alfresco, courtesy of a Michelin-starred chef, in the romantic summer garden of 17th-century Villa Bardini.

○ **Forte di Belvedere (p123)** Feasting on grandiose city panoramas from – and thought-provoking art installations in – this rambling fort.

○ **Lorenzo Villoresi (p126)** Take an interactive journey into the world of fragrances at this perfume museum.

Getting There

🚶 From Piazza della Stazione walk southeast along Via de' Panzani and Via de' Cerretani to the duomo. Head down Via Roma, cross Ponte Vecchio and continue south along Via Guicciardini to Palazzo Pitti.

🚌 Bus 13 runs to Piazzale Michelangelo.

Boboli & San Miniato al Monte Map on p120

Basilica di San Miniato al Monte (p122) KAVALENKAVA/SHUTTERSTOCK ©

Top Experience 📷
Set Foot in History in Palazzo Pitti

Wealthy banker Luca Pitti commissioned this palace in 1458, but once completed, waning family fortunes forced it to be sold to arch-rivals the Medici. It subsequently became home to the dukes of Lorraine and, when Florence was made capital of the nascent Kingdom of Italy in 1865, the Savoy (who gave it to the state in 1919).

◎ MAP P120, C3

☏ 055 29 48 83

www.uffizi.it/en/pitti-palace

adult/reduced Mar-Oct €16/8, Nov-Feb €10/5, combined ticket with Uffizi incl Giardino di Boboli Mar-Oct €38/21, Nov-Feb €18/11

🕔 8.15am-6.50pm Tue-Sun

Tesoro dei Granduchi

Exquisite amber carvings, ivory miniatures, glittering tiaras and headpieces, silver pillboxes and various other gems and jewels are displayed in the elaborately frescoed Grand Dukes' Treasury, on the ground floor of Palazzo Pitti. Notable (but not always open) is the **Sala di Giovanni da San Giovanni**, which sports lavish head-to-toe frescoes (1635–42) celebrating the life of Lorenzo Il Magnifico – spot Michelangelo giving Lorenzo a statue. 'Talk little, be brief and witty' is the curt motto above the painted staircase in the next room, the public audience chamber, where the grand duke received visitors in the presence of his court.

Galleria d'Arte Moderna

By 'modern', the Pitti's powers-that-be mean 18th and 19th century. So forget about Marini, Mertz or Clemente – the collection of this 2nd-floor gallery is dominated by late-19th-century works by artists of the Florentine Macchiaioli school (the local equivalent of impressionism), including Telemaco Signorini (1835–1901) and Giovanni Fattori (1825–1908).

Museo della Moda e del Costume

Pitti's **Fashion and Costume Museum** (adult/reduced incl Galleria Palatina, Appartamenti Reali & Galleria d'Arte Moderna Mar-Oct €16/8, Nov-Feb €10/5) plays host to various colourful temporary exhibitions, all with a strong fashion focus. If you're lucky, you might just get a chance to see some of the semi-decomposed burial clothes of Cosimo I (satin doublet and wool breeches), his wife Eleonora di Toledo (gown and silk stockings) and their son Don Garzia (doublet, beret and short cape). Considering they were buried for centuries, the historic garments are remarkably preserved.

★ Top Tips

o Ticketing for the palace complex and gardens comprises three options: Ticket 1 covers Palazzo Pitti (Galleria Palatina, Appartamenti Reali and Galleria d'Arte Moderna); Ticket 2 covers the Boboli Gardens (Giardino di Boboli, Giardino Bardini and Museo delle Porcellane); and Ticket 3 includes the previous two plus the Uffizi (single entry at each sight; valid three days). Buy from the ticket office by the palace entrance.

o Buy your Palazzo Pitti ticket before 8.59am and enter before 9.25am for a 50% reduction.

o Rent an audioguide (€8/13 for one/two people) at the ticket office.

✕ Take a Break

In summer, indulge in lunch at La Leggenda dei Frati (p124) in the gardens of Villa Bardini.

In winter, enjoy a classic Tuscan meal at family-run Da Ruggero (p125).

Appartamenti Reali

Accessed through the Galleria Palatina, these Royal Apartments are presented as they were c 1880–91 when the palace was occupied by members of the House of Savoy. The style and division of tasks assigned to each space is reminiscent of Spanish royal palaces, and all are heavily bedecked with drapes, silk and chandeliers.

Galleria Palatina

Raphaels and Rubens vie for centre stage in the enviable collection of 16th- to 18th-century art amassed by the Medici and Lorraine dukes in this art gallery, reached by several flights of stairs from the palace's central courtyard. This gallery has retained the original display arrangement of paintings (squeezed in, often on top of each other), so it can be visually overwhelming – go slow and focus on the works one by one.

Giardino di Boboli

Behind Palazzo Pitti, the Boboli Gardens were laid out in the mid-16th century to a design by architect Niccolò Pericoli. At the upper, southern limit, beyond the box-hedged rose garden, beautiful views over the Florentine countryside unfold. Much to the joy of many a local Florentine who can be found promenading in Boboli on a Sunday afternoon, Florence's homegrown fashion house Gucci has pledged €2 million to restore the gardens and their treasure trove of statues and fountains to their former pristine glory.

Galleria Palatina

The Palatina Art Collection

The gallery's highlights are found in a series of reception chambers dating from the Napoleonic period and decorated in the neoclassical style.

In the **Sala di Prometeo** is Fra' Filippo Lippi's *Madonna and Child with Stories from the Life of St Anne* (aka the Tondo Bartolini; 1452–53), one of the artist's major works. In the same room, admire the sombre *Madonna with Child and a Young St John the Baptist* (c 1490–95) by Botticelli. Its subject and execution stand in stark contrast to his earlier, often hedonistic, works – probably because it was painted after the death of Lorenzo the Magnificent, Botticelli's great patron, and during the ascendancy of the fire-and-brimstone preacher, Savonarola.

Madonna of the Window, named for the cloth-covered window in its background, is a charming work by Raphael, painted in 1513–14 towards the end of his glittering artistic career. Track the painting down in the **Sala di Ulisse**, once the bedroom of the Grand Dukes of Tuscany.

The gallery's sentimental favourite is undoubtedly Caravaggio's *Sleeping Cupid,* painted in 1608 in Malta, where the painter had fled after killing a man in a brawl and being exiled from Rome as a consequence. Find it in the **Sala dell'Educazione di Giove**.

The handsome **Sala dell'Iliade** showcases Raphael's *Portrait of a Woman* (aka *La Gravida*; c 1505–06) and the **Sala di Saturno** is home to his *Madonna with Child* and *St John the Baptist* (aka *The Madonna of the Chair*; 1511). Raphael's *Lady with a Veil* (aka *La Velata*; c 1516) holds court in the **Sala di Giove**.

The Venetian painter Titian (c 1490–1576) was a master of the portrait, and his painting of an unknown man (*Ritratto Virile*; c 1540–45) is one of his best. Known as *Portrait of a Man*, the subject displays a particularly piercing gaze. It's one of a number of Titians in the **Sala di Apollo**.

Museo delle Porcellane

Inside the 18th-century Palazzina del Cavaliere in the Boboli Gardens, this small museum houses an exquisite collection of European porcelain. Many pieces were brought to Florence from historic palaces in Parma, Piacenza and Sala Baganza in the late 19th century to decorate the Savoy family's Florentine residences.

Grotta del Buontalenti

Within the lower reaches of the gardens, don't miss this fantastical shell- and gem-encrusted *grotta,* a decorative grotto built by Bernardo Buontalenti between 1583 and 1593 for Francesco I de' Medici.

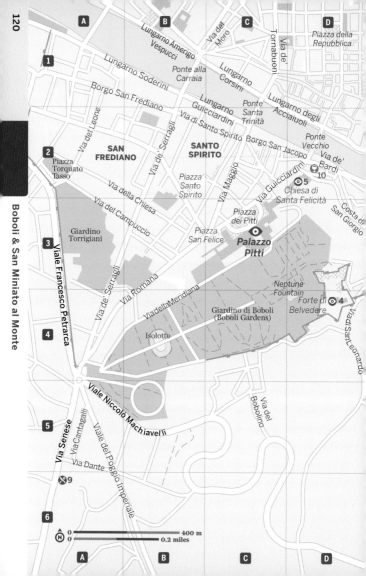

A
B
C
D

1

Via del Moro

Via del Tornabuoni

Piazza della Repubblica

Lungarno Amerigo Vespucci

Lungarno Soderini

Ponte alla Carraia

Lungarno Corsini

Borgo San Frediano

Lungarno Guicciardini

Ponte Santa Trinita

Lungarno degli Acciaiuoli

2

Via del Leone

Via de' Serragli

Via di Santo Spirito

Borgo San Jacopo

Ponte Vecchio

Via de' Bardi

SAN FREDIANO

SANTO SPIRITO

Piazza Torquato Tasso

Via della Chiesa

Piazza Santo Spirito

Via Maggio

Via Guicciardini

Chiesa di Santa Felicità

10

5

Piazza dei Pitti

Costa di San Giorgio

3

Via del Campuccio

Giardino Torrigiani

Piazza San Felice

Palazzo Pitti

Viale Francesco Petrarca

Via Romana

Via de' Serragli

Viadella Meridiana

Neptune Fountain

Forte di Belvedere

4

Via di San Leonardo

4

Giardino di Boboli (Boboli Gardens)

Isolotto

5

Viale Niccolò Machiavelli

Via Senese

Via Cantagalli

Viale del Poggio Imperiale

Via Dante

Via del Bobolino

9

6

N

0   400 m
0   0.2 miles

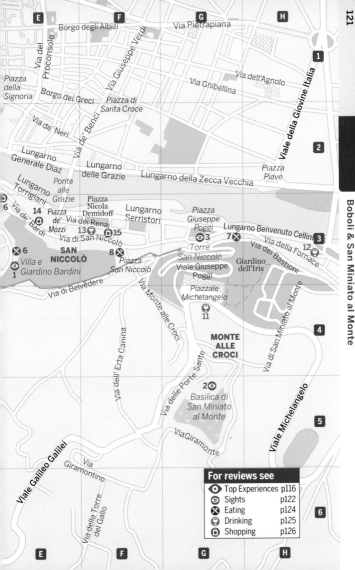

Borgo degli Albizi

Via Pietrapiana

Via del Proconsolo

Via Giuseppe Verdi

Via dell'Agnolo

Via Ghibellina

Via della Giovine Italia

Piazza della Signoria

Borgo dei Greci

Piazza di Santa Croce

Via de' Benci

Via de' Neri

Lungarno Generale Diaz

Lungarno delle Grazie

Lungarno della Zecca Vecchia

Piazza Piave

Ponte alle Grazie

Lungarno Torrigiani

Via de' Bardi

14 Piazza de' Mozzi

Piazza Nicola Demidoff

Lungarno Serristori

Via de' Renai

13 **15**

Via di San Niccolò

Piazza Giuseppe Poggi

3

Lungarno Benvenuto Cellini

7

Via della Fornace

12

Via dei Bastioni

6

Villa e Giardino Bardini

1

SAN NICCOLÒ

8 Piazza San Niccolò

Torre San Niccolò

Viale Giuseppe Poggi

Giardino dell'Iris

Via di Belvedere

Via Monte alle Croci

Piazzale Michelangelo

11

Via di San Miniato al Monte

Via dell'Erta Canina

MONTE ALLE CROCI

Via delle Porte Sante

2

Basilica di San Miniato al Monte

Viale Michelangelo

Viale Galileo Galilei

Via Giramontino

ViaGiramonte

Via della Torre del Gallo

For reviews see	
⊙ Top Experiences	p116
⊙ Sights	p122
⊗ Eating	p124
⊙ Drinking	p125
⊙ Shopping	p126

Sights

Villa e
Giardino Bardini

GARDENS

1 ◉ MAP P120, E3

This 17th-century villa and garden was named after 19th-century antiquarian art collector Stefano Bardini (1836–1922), who bought it in 1913 and restored its ornamental medieval garden. It has all the features of a quintessential Tuscan garden, including artificial grottoes, orangery, marble statues and fountains. Inside the villa, the small **Museo Pietro Annigoni** displays works by Italian painter Pietro Annigoni (1910–88). End with city views from the romantic roof terrace. (☎ 055 2006 6233; www.villabardini.it; Costa San Giorgio 2, Via de' Bardi 1r; adult/reduced villa €10/5, gardens €6/3, gardens with Giardino di Boboli ticket free; ⊙ villa 10am-7pm Tue-Sun, gardens 8.15am-7.30pm summer, shorter hours winter, closed 1st & last Mon of month)

Basilica di San
Miniato al Monte

CHURCH

2 ◉ MAP P120, G5

Five minutes' walk uphill from Piazzale Michelangelo is this wonderful Romanesque church, dedicated to St Minius, an early Christian martyr in Florence said to have flown to this spot after his death down in the town (or, if you want to believe an alternative version, walked up the hill with his head tucked underneath his arm). The church dates from

Forte di Belvedere

the early 11th century, although its typical Tuscan multicoloured marble facade was tacked on a couple of centuries later. (☏055 234 27 31; www.sanminiatoalmonte.it; Via Monte alle Croci; admission free; ◷9.30am-1pm & 3-7.30pm summer, to 7pm winter)

Torre San Niccolò
GATE

3 ◉ MAP P120, G3

Built in 1324, the best preserved of the city's medieval gates stands sentinel on the banks of the Arno. In summer, with a guide you can scale the steep stairs inside the tower to enjoy blockbuster river and city views. Visits organised by Muse Firenze (p54) are limited to 15 people at a time (no children under eight years) and advance reservations are essential; book online, by email or by phone. Tours are cancelled when it rains. (☏055 276 85 58, 055 276 82 24; www.muse firenze.it; Piazza Giuseppe Poggi; guided visit every 30min €4; ◷5-8pm late Jun-late Sep)

Forte di Belvedere
FORTRESS

4 ◉ MAP P120, D4

Forte di Belvedere is a rambling fort designed by Bernardo Buontalenti for Grand Duke Ferdinando I at the end of the 16th century. From the massive bulwark, soldiers kept watch on four fronts – as much for internal security as to protect the Palazzo Pitti against foreign attack. Today the fort hosts summertime art exhibitions, which are well worth a peek if only to

Piazzale Michelangelo

Turn your back on the bevy of ticky-tacky souvenir stalls flogging David statues and boxer shorts and take in the spectacular city panorama from this vast square, pierced by one of Florence's two *David* copies. Sunset here is particularly dramatic. It's a 10-minute uphill walk along the serpentine road, paths and steps that scale the hillside from the Arno and Piazza Giuseppe Poggi; from Piazza San Niccolò walk uphill and bear left up the long flight of steps signposted Viale Michelangelo. Or take bus 13 from Stazione di Santa Maria Novella.

revel in the sweeping city panorama that can be had from the fort. Outside of exhibition times, the fort is closed. (Via di San Leonardo 1; admission free; ◷hours vary)

Chiesa di Santa Felicità
CHURCH

5 ◉ MAP P120, D2

Possibly founded by Syrian merchants as early as the 2nd century, the current church is largely a Renaissance construction. Its most extraordinary feature is Brunelleschi's small Cappella Barbadori, which is adorned with frescoes by Jacopo Pontormo (1494–1557) of the *Annunciation* and a *Deposition from the Cross*,

Summer Hang-out

The enormous car-free, paved terrace fronting Palazzo Pitti is the hot spot in warm weather to lounge on the ground and chill with friends; sunset colours the entire vast facade of Palazzo Pitti a dazzling pink.

in garish reds, pinks and oranges. The Corridoio Vasariano (p52) passes right across the facade so the Medici could hear Mass like any good Christians, but without having to mix with the common folk. (Piazza di Santa Felicità; ⏰9.30am-noon & 3.30-5.30pm Mon-Sat)

Eating

La Leggenda dei Frati
TUSCAN €€€

6 ✘ MAP P120, E3

Summertime's hottest address. At home in the grounds of historic Villa Bardini, Michelin-starred Legend of Friars enjoys the most romantic terrace with a view in Florence. Veggies are plucked fresh from the vegetable patch, tucked between waterfalls and ornamental beds in Giardino Bardini, and contemporary art jazzes up the classically chic interior. Cuisine is Tuscan, gastronomic and well worth the vital advance reservation. (📞055 068 05 45; www.laleggendadeifrati.it; Villa Bardini,

Costa di San Giorgio 6a; menus €105 & €130, meals €90; ⏰12.30-2pm & 7.30-10pm Tue-Sun; 📶)

La Bottega del Buon Caffè
TUSCAN €€€

7 ✘ MAP P120, G3

Farm to table is the philosophy of this Michelin-starred restaurant where head chef Antonello Sardi mesmerises diners from the stunning open kitchen. Veg and herbs arrive from the restaurant's own farm, Borgo Santo Pietro, in the Sienese hills. Breads and focaccia (the nut version is heavenly) are homemade and the olive oil used (special production from Vinci) is clearly only the best. (📞055 553 56 77; www.borgointhecity.com; Lungarno Benvenuto Cellini 69r; meals from €80; ⏰7.30-10.30pm Mon, 12.30-3pm & 7.30-10.30pm Tue-Sat; 📶)

ZEB
TUSCAN €€

8 ✘ MAP P120, F3

Local gastronomes adore this modern, minimalist address with five-star wine list at the foot of the hill leading up to Piazzale Michelangelo, in village-like San Niccolò. Post-panorama, sit around the deli-style counter and indulge in a delicious choice of cold cuts and creative Tuscan dishes prepared by passionate chef Alberto Navari and his *mamma* Giuseppina. (📞055 234 28 64; www.zebgastronomia.com; Via San Miniato 2r; meals €35; ⏰12.30-3pm & 7.30-10.30pm Thu-Tue, closed Mon-Wed winter)

Da Ruggero

TUSCAN €€

9 MAP P120, A6

A 10-minute stroll through Boboli Gardens (or along the street from Porta Romana) uncovers this trattoria, run by the gracious Corsi family since 1981 and much loved for its pure, unadulterated Florentine tradition. Cuisine is Tuscan simple and hearty – *zuppa di ortiche* (nettle soup), *spaghetti alla carrettiera* (spaghetti in a chilli-fired tomato sauce) and, of course, the iconic *bistecca* (T-bone steak). (📞055 22 05 42; Via Senese 89r; meals €25; ⏰noon-2.30pm & 7-10.30pm Thu-Mon, closed mid-Jul–mid-Aug)

Drinking

Le Volpi e l'Uva

WINE BAR

10 MAP P120, D2

This humble wine bar remains as appealing as the day it opened in 1992. Its food and wine pairings are first class – taste and buy boutique wines by small Italian producers, matched perfectly with cheeses, cold meats and the finest crostini in town; the warm, melt-in-your-mouth *lardo di cinta senese* (wafer-thin slices of aromatic pork fat) is absolutely extraordinary.

There are wine-tasting classes too – or simply work your way through the impressive 50-odd different wines available by the glass (€4.50 to €9). (📞055 239 81 32;

Street Art in Oltrarno: Clet

➡️🔖

Should you notice something gone awry with street signs in Oltrarno – on a No Entry sign, a tiny black figure stealthily sneaking away with the white bar for example – you can be sure it is the work of French-born Clet Abraham, one of Florence's most popular street artists. In his Oltrarno **studio** (📞339 2203607, 347 3387760; Via dell'Olmo 8r; ⏰hours vary) you can buy stickers and postcards featuring his hacked traffic signs and, if you're lucky, catch a glimpse of the rebellious artist at work.

In 2011 Clet created quite a stir in his adopted city by installing, in the black of night, a life-sized figurine entitled *Uomo Comune* (*Common Man*) on Ponte alle Grazie (to which the city authorities turned a blind eye for a week before removing it). Should you fall completely and utterly head over heels in love with Clet's work, you can either order a reproduction street sign directly from his workshop (from €500) or purchase an original (numbered and signed, from €2500) limited edition from Mio Concept (p73) – Clet produces only 13 of each design.

Summer Clubbing

The hottest and hippest place to be seen in the city on hot sultry summer nights is **Flò** (☑ 334 1080164, 334 1080164 055 65 07 91; www.flofirenze. com; Piazzale Michelangelo 84; ⏱7.30pm-4am late May-Sep), a truly ab fab seasonal lounge bar that pops up each May or June on Piazzale Michelangelo. There are different themed lounge areas, a dance floor and a VIP area (where you have no chance of reserving a table unless you're in the Florentine in-crowd).

www.levolpieluva.com; Piazza dei Rossi 1; ⏱11am-9pm Mon-Sat)

La Loggia   CAFE

11 ⬤ MAP P120, G4

With one of Florence's finest terraces overlooking the city from its hilltop perch, this historic cafe is predictably prime real estate. At home in an elegant 19th-century lodge once intended to house the sculptures of local lad Michelangelo, La Loggia serves drinks and light snacks beneath its vintage stone arches and classic Tuscan cuisine in its upmarket restaurant (meals around €50). (☑ 055 234 28 32; www.ristorantelaloggia.it; Piazzale Michelangelo 1; ⏱11am-11pm; 🛜)

Surf Ventura   COCKTAIL BAR

12 ⬤ MAP P120, H3

If a scooped-out papaya filled with alcohol is your cup of tea or you fancy a bespoke cocktail crafted especially for you by the eminently charming owner and mixologist Mauro, hit this underground cocktail club. Look for the hefty iron door, ring the bell, fill in a membership form if you don't have one, and descend down the staircase to cocktail heaven. (☑ 055 68 85 89; Via Ser Ventura Monachi 21r; ⏱9.30pm-2am Wed-Mon)

Zoé   BAR

13 ⬤ MAP P120, F3

This savvy Oltrarno old-timer knows exactly what its hip punters want – a relaxed, faintly industrial space to hang out in all hours (well, almost). Be it breakfast, lunch, cocktails or after-dinner party, Zoé is your gal. Come springtime's warmth, the scene spills out onto a wooden decked street terrace out the front. (☑ 055 24 31 11; www. zoeflorence.com; Via dei Renai 13r; ⏱8am-3am; 🛜)

Shopping

Lorenzo Villoresi   PERFUME

14 🔒 MAP P120, E3

Artisanal perfumes, bodycare products, scented candles and stones, essential oils and room fragrances crafted by Florentine perfumer Lorenzo Villoresi meld distinctively Tuscan elements such as laurel, olive, cypress and iris with essential oils and essences from around the world. His bespoke fragrances are highly sought after and visiting his elegant boutique, at home in his family's 15th-century *palazzo*, is quite an experience. (055 234 11 87; www.lorenzovilloresi.it; Via de' Bardi 14; 10am-7pm Mon-Sat)

Marco Baroni   JEWELLERY

15 MAP P120, F3

Duck into this old-fashioned atelier to watch revered Florentine goldsmith Marco Baroni at work. Using all types of gold as well as iron, he crafts exquisite rings, bracelets, pendants and earrings embedded with rare, precious and semi-precious gems and stones. His

attention to detail – all his pieces feature intricate engraving – is remarkable. (055 246 90 32; www. marcobaronifirenze.com; Via dei Renai 3; 9.30am-1pm & 3.30-7pm)

Il Torchio   ARTS & CRAFTS

16 MAP P120, E3

Peek into Erin Ciulla's workshop for a contemporary insight into traditional Florentine bookbinding. Among the treasure trove of gifts to buy are hand-sewn leather books, marbled-paper photo frames and journals in the shape of musical instruments. Personalised items can be ordered in advance. (055 234 28 62; www. legatoriailtorchio.com; Via de' Bardi 17; 10am-1.30pm & 2.30-7pm Mon-Fri, 10am-1pm Sat)

Shops on the Ponte Vecchio (p134)

Explore ✦

Oltrarno

Literally the 'other side of the Arno', this atmospheric neighbourhood is the traditional home of the city's artisans and its streets are peppered with botteghe (workshops), designer boutiques and hybrid forms of both. Food and drink is also a strength – prepared using artisanal ingredients, of course – and there's an ever-growing number of fashionable restaurants and bars to lure you across the river.

The Short List

○ **Cappella Brancacci (p132)** Getting lost in the exquisite detail of 13th-century frescoes inside this bijou backstreet chapel.

○ **Giardino Torrigiani (p133)** Enjoying a private tour of the city's most beautiful walled garden.

○ **Ponte Vecchio (p134)** Feasting on romantic views of Florence splayed out either side of the Arno river; sunset is sensational.

○ **Mad Souls & Spirits (p137)** Mingling with cocktail creatives and discovering Florence's exciting cocktail scene at this uber-cool San Frediano hang-out.

○ **Enoteca Pitti Gola e Cantina (p139)** Indulging in an exceptional wine flight and learning about Tuscan wines with a knowledgeable sommelier.

Getting There

🚶 From Piazza della Stazione walk southeast to the Duomo. From Via Roma, cross the Ponte Vecchio and you're in Oltrarno.

Oltrarno Map on p130

Arno river and Oltrarno KAVALENKAVA/SHUTTERSTOCK ©

A

B

C

D

1

17

Lungarno di Santa Rosa

Ponte
Amerigo
Vespucci

Lungarno Amerigo Vespucci

Piazza
d'Ognissanti

2

Piazza
di Verzaia

30 **14**

Piazza di
Cestello

4

Lungarno Soderini

11

Via San Giovanni

Via Sant'Onofrio

Piazza
dei Nerli

Borgo San Frediano

18 **22**

**SAN
FREDIANO**

Via Ludovico Ariosto

Via del Drago d'Oro

Via del Leone

3

7

Via dell'Orto

Piazza del
Carmine

Borgo della Stella

24

Piazza
Piattellina

1

Via Santa Monaca

Cappella
Brancacci

12

Via dell'Ardiglione

28

Via di Camaldoli

Via del Leone

4

Piazza
Torquato
Tasso

Via della Chiesa

25

Via de' Serragli

Via della Chies

5

Viale Francesco Petrarca

Via del Campuccio

Giardino
Torrigiani

Via del Campuccio

Via Santa Maria

6

A

B

C

D

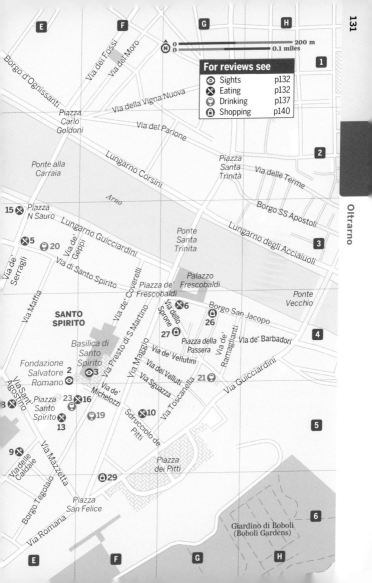

E — F — G — H

Via dei Fossi
Via del Moro
Borgo d'Ognissanti

For reviews see
- Sights p132
- Eating p132
- Drinking p137
- Shopping p140

N 0 ———————— 200 m
0 ———————— 0.1 miles

1

Piazza
Carlo
Goldoni

Via della Vigna Nuova

Via del Parione

Piazza
Santa
Trinità

Via delle Terme

2

Ponte alla
Carraia

Lungarno Corsini

Arno

Borgo SS Apostoli

Oltrarno

15 Piazza
N Sauro

Lungarno Guicciardini

Ponte
Santa
Trinita

Lungarno degli Acciaiuoli

3

5 20

Via de' Geppi
Via di Santo Spirito

Via de' Coverelli
Piazza de'
Frescobaldi

Palazzo
Frescobaldi

Ponte
Vecchio

Via de' Serragli
Via Mattia

SANTO
SPIRITO

Via de' Presto di S.Martino

Via della
Sprone
6
27

Borgo San Jacopo
26

Piazza della
Passera

Via de' Ramaglianti
Via de' Barbadori

4

Fondazione
Salvatore
Romano

Basilica di
Santo
Spirito
2
3

Via Maggio
Via de' Vellutini

Via de' Velluti

Via de' Guicciardini
21

Via Sant'Agostino

Piazza
Santo
Spirito
23 16
13

Via de' Michelozzi

Via Sguazza

Via Toscanella

Sdrucciolo de'
Pitti

10

19

5

9

Via delle
Caldaie

Via Mazzetta

Piazza
dei Pitti

Borgo Tegolaio

29

Piazza
San Felice

Via Romana

Giardino di Boboli
(Boboli Gardens)

6

E — F — G — H

Sights

Cappella Brancacci
CHAPEL

1 ◉ MAP P130, C4

Fire in the 18th century practically destroyed 13th-century **Basilica di Santa Maria del Carmine** (Piazza del Carmine; ☉6.15am-noon & 5-6.45pm Mon-Sat, 9.15am-1pm & 5-7pm Sun), but it spared its magnificent chapel frescoes – a treasure of paintings by Masolino da Panicale, Masaccio and Filippino Lippi commissioned by rich merchant Felice Brancacci upon his return from Egypt in 1423. The chapel entrance is right of the main church entrance. Only 30 people can visit at a time, limited to 30 minutes in high season; pricier weekend tickets include admission to the Fondazione Salvatore Romano. (☎055 238 21 95; www.museicivicifiorentini.comune.fi.it; Piazza del Carmine 14; adult/reduced Wed-Fri €8/6, Sat-Mon €10/7; ☉10am-5pm Wed-Sat & Mon, 1-5pm Sun)

Fondazione Salvatore Romano
MUSEUM

2 ◉ MAP P130, E4

For a change of pace from the Renaissance, head to this Gothic-style former refectory safeguarding an imposing wall fresco by Andrea Orcagna depicting the Last Supper and the Crucifixion (c 1370), one of the largest 14th-century paintings to survive. The museum itself displays a collection of rare 11th-century Romanesque sculpture, paintings and antique furniture donated to the city by art collector and antiquarian Salvatore Romano (1875–1955). Tickets are sold at Cappella Brancacci; one ticket covers admission to both sights. (Cenacolo di Santo Spirito; ☎055 28 70 43; www.musei civicifiorentini.comune.fi.it; Piazza Santo Spirito 29; adult/reduced €10/7; ☉10am-4pm Sat-Mon)

Basilica di Santo Spirito
CHURCH

3 ◉ MAP P130, F4

The facade of this Brunelleschi church, on Florence's most shabby-chic piazza, makes a striking backdrop to open-air concerts in summer. Inside, the basilica's length is lined with 38 semicircular chapels (covered with a plain wall in the 1960s), and a colonnade of grey pietra forte Corinthian columns injects monumental grandeur. Artworks to look for include Domenico di Zanobi's Madonna of the Relief (1485) in the Cappella Velutti, in which the Madonna wards off a little red devil with a club. (www.basilicasantospirito.it; Piazza Santo Spirito; ☉8.30am-1pm & 3-6pm Mon, Tue & Thu-Sat, 11.30am-1.30pm & 3-6pm Sun)

Eating

Essenziale
TUSCAN €€€

4 ✕ MAP P130, C2

There's no finer showcase for modern Tuscan cuisine than this loft-style restaurant in a 19th-century warehouse. Preparing dishes at the kitchen bar in rolled-up shirt sleeves and navy butcher's apron is dazzling young chef Simone Cipriani. Order one of his tasting menus to sample the full range of his inventive, thoroughly modern cuisine inspired by classic Tuscan dishes. (☏ 055 247 69 56; www.essenziale.me; Piazza di Cestello 3r; 6-/8-course tasting menu €65/80; ☺ 7-10pm Tue-Sat; 📶)

Il Santo Bevitore
TUSCAN €€

5 ✖ MAP P130, E3

Reserve or arrive right on 7.30pm to snag the last table at this ever-popular address, an ode to stylish dining where gastronomes eat by candlelight in a vaulted, whitewashed, bottle-lined interior. The menu is a creative reinvention of seasonal classics: pumpkin gnocchi with hazelnuts, coffee and green-veined *blu di Capra* (goat's-milk cheese), *tagliatelle* with hare *ragù*, garlic cream and sweet Carmignano figs. (☏ 055 21 12 64; www.ilsantobevitore.com; Via di Santo Spirito 64-66r; meals €40; ☺ 12.30-2.30pm & 7.30-11.30pm, closed Sun lunch & Aug)

Cammillo
TRATTORIA €€€

6 ✖ MAP P130, G4

Crostini topped with aphrodisiacal white-truffle shavings, deep-fried zucchini (courgette) flowers or artichokes and homemade walnut liqueur are a few of the seasonal highlights served beneath a

A Secret Garden

Vast secret **Giardino Torrigiani** (☏ 055 22 45 27; www.giardinotorrigiani.it; Via de' Serragli 144; 1½hr guided tours by donation; ☺ advance reservation via email) is Europe's largest privately owned green space within a historic centre and can be visited with the charismatic Marquis Vanni Torrigiani Malaspina and his wife, Susanna.

Designed during the Romantic movement in the early 19th century, the garden frames the original 16th-century villa and later 19th-century house. Admire rare tree species, a beautifully restored greenhouse and city walls built under Cosimo I in 1544 (one of six sets of walls to be built around Florence at different times).

centuries-old red-brick vaulted ceiling at this veteran trattoria, a Florentine landmark since 1945.

Prices feel elevated and service can be slow, but the quality of products used is exceptional. (☏ 055 21 24 27; Borgo San Jacopo 57r; meals €50; ☺ noon-2.30pm & 7.30-10.30pm Thu-Mon)

Burro e Acciughe
TUSCAN €€

7 ✖ MAP P130, B3

Carefully sourced, quality ingredients drive this tiny trattoria that

Ponte Vecchio

Dating to 1345, **Ponte Vecchio** was the only Florentine bridge to survive destruction at the hands of retreating German forces in 1944. Above the jewellers' shops on the eastern side, the Corridoio Vasariano (Vasari Corridor) is a 16th-century passageway between the Uffizi and Palazzo Pitti that runs around, rather than through, the medieval Torre dei Mannelli at the bridge's southern end. The first documentation of a stone bridge here, at the narrowest crossing point along the entire length of the Arno, dates from 972.

Floods in 1177 and 1333 destroyed the bridge, and in 1966 it came close to being destroyed again. Many of the jewellers with shops on the bridge were convinced the floodwaters would sweep away their livelihoods; fortunately, the bridge held.

They're still here. Indeed, the bridge has twinkled with the glittering wares of jewellers, their trade often passed down from generation to generation, ever since the 16th century, when Ferdinando I de' Medici ordered them here to replace the often malodorous presence of the town butchers, who used to toss unwanted leftovers into the river.

woos punters with a short but stylish choice of raw (tartare and carpaccio) and cooked fish dishes. The gnocchi topped with octopus *ragù* (stew) is out of this world, as is the *baccalà* (salted cod) with creamed leeks, turnip and deep-fried polenta wedges. Excellent wine list too. (Butter & Anchovies; ☎ 055 045 72 86; www.facebook.com/burroeacciughe; Via dell'Orto 35; meals €35; ⊙ 7-11.45pm Tue-Fri, noon-2pm & 7pm-midnight Sat & Sun)

#Raw

VEGAN €

8 ⊗ MAP P130, E5

Should you desire a turmeric, ginger or aloe vera shot or a gently warmed, raw vegan burger served on a stylish slate-and-wood plat-

ter, innovative Raw hits the spot. Everything served here is freshly made and raw – to sensational effect. Herbs are grown in the biodynamic greenhouse of charismatic and hugely knowledgeable chef Caroline, a Swedish architect before moving to Florence. (☎ 055 21 93 79; www.hashtagraw.it; Via Sant'Agostino 11r; meals €8-15; ⊙ 10am-6pm Tue-Fri, 11am-8pm Sat & Sun; 🛜 ✐)

Gurdulù

RISTORANTE €€

9 ⊗ MAP P130, E5

Gourmet Gurdulù seduces fashionable Florentines with razor-sharp interior design, magnificent craft cocktails and seasonal market cuisine from young local chef Gabriele Andreoni. A hybrid drink-dine, this address is as much about noshing gourmet *aperitivi* snacks over expertly mixed cocktails (€12) or an expertly curated Tuscan wine flight (€25 for four wines) as it is about dining exceedingly well. (☏055 28 22 23; www.gurdulu.com; Via delle Caldaie 12r; meals €40, tasting menu €55; ☺7.30-11pm Tue-Sat, 12.30-2.30pm & 7.30-11pm Sun; ☏)

Carduccio VEGAN €

10 ❌ MAP P130, F5

With just a handful of tables, this *salotto bio* (organic living room) oozes intimacy. Miniature cabbage 'flowers' decorate each table, fruit and veg crates stack up by the bar, and the menu is 100% organic. Knock back an energising ginger, lemon and turmeric shot (€3) or linger over delicious salads, quiches, soups, poke bowls and vegan burgers.

Between meals, a superb choice of cold-pressed juices, smoothies and super-smoothies rule the healthy roost. (☏055 238 20 70; www.facebook.com/carducciofirenze; Sdrucciolo de Pitti 10r; meals €8-15; ☺8am-8pm Mon-Sat, 10am-5pm Sun; ☏)

iO Osteria Personale TUSCAN €€

11 ❌ MAP P130, A2

Persuade everyone at your table to order the tasting menu to avoid the torture of picking just one dish – everything on the menu at this fabulously contemporary and creative *osteria* is to die for. Pontedera-born chef Nicolò Baretti uses only seasonal products, natural ingredients and traditional flavours – to sensational effect. (☏055 933 13 41; www.io-osteria personale.it; Borgo San Frediano 167r; 4-/5-/6-course tasting menus €40/49/57; ☺7.30-10pm Mon-Sat)

S.Forno BAKERY €

12 ❌ MAP P130, D4

Shop at this hipster bakery, around for at least a century, for fresh breads and pastries baked to sweet perfection in its ancient *forno* (oven) by local baker Angelo. Gourmet dried products stack

Piazza della Passera 🍽️

This bijou square with no passing traffic is a gourmet gem. Pick from cheap wholesome tripe in various guises at **Il Magazzino** (☏055 21 59 69; Piazza della Passera 2/3; meals €40; ☺noon-3pm & 7.30-11pm); vegetarian at **5 e Cinque** (☏055 274 15 83; www.5ecinque. it; Piazza della Passera 1; meals €25; ☺noon-3pm & 7.30-10pm Tue-Sun; ☏); or upmarket Tuscan classics at veteran address **Trattoria 4 Leoni** (☏055 21 85 62; www.4leoni. com; Via de' Vellutini 1r; meals €50; ☺noon-midnight), known for its brilliantly blue *bistecca alla fiorentina* cooked up since 1550.

Summer Concerts

Watch for open-air concerts, film screenings and other edgy, summertime cultural happenings on Piazza Santo Spirito.

up on vintage shelves, and it also cooks up old-fashioned breakfasts (milk and biscuits!), soups, quiches and bespoke *panini* (€4 to €6) too, to eat in or out. (☑ 055 239 85 80; www.facebook.com/sfornofirenze; Via Santa Monaco 3r; ⏱ 7.30am-7.30pm Mon-Fri, from 8am Sat & Sun)

Tamerò
ITALIAN €€

13 ⊗ MAP P130, E5

A happening pasta bar on Florence's hippest square: admire chefs at work in the open kitchen while you wait for a table. A buoyant, party-loving crowd flocks here to fill up on imaginative fresh pasta (€9 to €14), giant salads and copious cheese and salami platters. Decor is trendy industrial, *aperitivo* 'happy hour' (€11) is 6.30pm to 8.30pm, and weekend DJs spin sets from 10pm. (☑ 055 28 25 96; www.tamero.it; Piazza Santo Spirito 11r; meals €25; ⏱ noon-3pm & 6.30pm-2am Tue-Sun; 🛜)

All'Antico Ristoro di' Cambi
TUSCAN €€

14 ⊗ MAP P130, B2

Founded as a wine shop in 1950, this Oltrarno institution sticks closely to the traditional, with its long list of fine Tuscan wines and dried meats hanging from beautiful red-brick-vaulted ceilings. This is one of the best places in town to try both traditional Roman deep-fried artichokes and Florence's iconic T-bone steak (€45 per kilogram).

Meat aficionados will also enjoy the succulent *tagliata di cinta senese* (Senese pork steak) and *ossobuco all fiorentina* (veal shank in a tomato and wine sauce). (☑ 055 21 71 34; www.anticoristoro dicambi.it; Via Sant'Onofrio 1r; meals €35; ⏱ noon-2.30pm & 6-10.30pm Mon-Sat)

Gelateria La Carraia
GELATO €

15 ⊗ MAP P130, E3

One glance at the constant line out the door of this bright green-and-citrus shop with exciting flavours (ricotta and pear, strawberry cheesecake, walnut and fig, the best mint in town) and you'll know you're at a Florentine favourite. (☑ 055 28 06 95; www.lacarraiagroup.eu; Piazza Nazario Sauro 25r; cones & tubs €1.50-6; ⏱ 11am-midnight)

Trattoria Gustapanino
ITALIAN €

16 ⊗ MAP P130, F5

With tables beneath parasols bang-slap on enchanting Piazza Santo Spirito and a traditional Tuscan kitchen that churns out the classics pretty much all day, Gustapanino can do no wrong. The wooden tables inside its bottle-lined interior are constantly packed – occasionally to the detriment of good service – and visitors love it. Well-stuffed *panini* (€4.50 to €7) to go too. (055 28 92 30; www.facebook.com/gusta-panino; Piazza Santo Spirito 1; meals €15-25; 10.30am-midnight Tue-Sun, from 4.30pm Mon summer)

Drinking

Santarosa Bistrot BAR

17 MAP P130, A1

The living is easy at this hipster garden-bistro-bar, snug against a chunk of ancient city wall in the flowery Santarosa gardens. Comfy cushioned sofas built from recycled wooden crates sit alfresco beneath trees; food is superb (meals €30); and mixologists behind the

bar complement an excellent wine list curated by Enoteca Pitti Gola e Cantina (p139) with serious craft cocktails. (055 230 90 57; www.facebook.com/santarosa.bistrot; Lungarno di Santarosa; 8am-midnight;)

Mad Souls & Spirits COCKTAIL BAR

18 MAP P130, D3

At this ubercool bar in San Frediano, cult alchemists Neri Fantechi and Julian Biondi woo a discerning crowd with their expertly crafted cocktails, served in a tiny aqua-green and red-brick space that couldn't be more spartan. A potted cactus decorates each scrubbed wood table and the humorous cocktail menu is the height of

Piazza Santo Spirito

CHRISTIAN MUELLER/SHUTTERSTOCK ©

irreverence. Check the 'Daily Madness' blackboard for specials. (📞055 627 16 21; www.facebook.com/madsoulsandspirits; Borgo San Frediano 38r; ⏰6pm-2am; 📶)

Rasputin
COCKTAIL BAR

19 🍸 MAP P130, F5

The 'secret' speakeasy everyone knows about, it has no sign outside: disguised as a chapel of sorts, look for the tiny entrance with the two-seat wooden pew, crucifix on the wall, vintage pics and tea lights flickering in the doorway. Inside, it's back to the 1930s with period furnishings, an exclusive vibe and bar staff mixing Prohibition-era cocktails.

Cocktail Culture

There is no finer neighbourhood for hobnobbing with fashionable Florentines over craft cocktails than trendy **San Frediano** in the Oltrarno; top spots include Mad Souls & Spirits (p137), 'secret' speakeasy Rasputin and Balkan-influenced Gurdulù (p134). For creative sake-based fusion cocktails in the company of Japanese tapas, head to smart Japanese cocktail bar **Kawaii** (📞055 28 14 00; www.momoyamakawaii.it; Borgo San Frediano 8r; ⏰12.30-2.30pm & 6.30pm-1.30am Tue-Sat, 6.30pm-1.30am Sun).

Table reservations (via phone or Facebook page) recommended. (📞055 28 03 99; www.facebook.com/rasputinfirenze; Borgo Tegolaio 21r; ⏰8pm-2am)

Il Santino
WINE BAR

20 🍸 MAP P130, E3

Kid sister to top-notch restaurant Il Santo Bevitore (p133) two doors down the same street, this intimate wine bar with exposed stone walls and marble bar is a stylish spot for pairing cured meats, cheeses and Tuscan staples with a carefully curated selection of wine – many by local producers – and artisanal beers. (📞055 230 28 20; http://ilsantobevitore.com; Via di Santo Spirito 60r; ⏰12.30-11pm)

Ditta Artigianale
CAFE, BAR

21 ☕ MAP P130, G4

The second branch of Florence's premier coffee roaster (p112) treats its faithful hipster clientele to full-blown dining in a 1950s-styled interior alongside its signature speciality coffees and a laid-back vibe. Think bright geometric-patterned wall-paper, comfy gold and pea-green armchairs, a mezzanine bistro up top, buzzing ground-floor bar below, and tiny street terrace out the back.

Watch for barista-run coffee workshops and tastings. Brunch (€9 to €19), served from 9am to 6pm, translates as fantastic pancakes, pastries, eggs in every guise, maple-syrup-soaked French toast, muesli bowls and so forth. Feisty burgers and club sandwiches (€8 to €12) dominate the lunchtime kitchen. (📞 055 045 71 63; www.dittaartigianale.it; Via dello Sprone 5r; 🕒 8am-midnight Mon-Fri, from 9am Sat & Sun; 📶)

La Cité
BAR

22 🚇 MAP P130, D3

A hip cafe-bookshop with an eclectic choice of vintage seating, La Cité makes a wonderful, intimate venue for book readings, after-work drinks and fantastic live music, including jazz, swing and world music. Check its Facebook page for the week's events. (www.facebook.com/lacitelibreriacafe; Borgo San Frediano 20r; 🕒 10am-2am Mon-Sat, from 2pm Sun; 📶)

Volume
BAR

23 🚇 MAP P130, E5

Armchairs, recycled and upcycled vintage furniture, books to read, jukebox, crêpes and a tasty choice of nibbles with coffee or a light lunch give this hybrid cafe-bar-gallery real appeal – all in an old hat-making workshop with tools and wooden moulds strewn around. Watch for various music, art and DJ events and other happenings.

Good-value drinks are served during *aperitivi* each evening from 6.30pm to 10pm. (📞 055 238 14 60; www.volumefirenze.com; Piazza Santo Spirito 3r; 🕒 8.30am-1am Sun-Tue, to 1.30am Thu-Sat)

Wine Tasting

If you're in Tuscany for the wine, an evening of tastings over dinner with expert and incredibly entertaining sommeliers Edoardo, Manuele and Zeno at **Enoteca Pitti Gola e Cantina** (📞 055 21 27 04; www.pittigolaecantina.com; Piazza dei Pitti 16; 🕒 1pm-midnight Wed-Mon) is an essential. Floor-to-ceiling shelves of expertly curated, small-production Tuscan and Italian wines fill the tiny bar and casual dining (excellent cured meats, homemade pasta) is around a handful of marble-topped tables.

Exceptional wine tastings range from simple wine flights (three wines €20) to lunch tastings (four wines with lunch €35) and a full-blown evening of tastings over dinner (15 to 20 wines €160, weekends only). Reservations are essential. The team has its own fully fledged restaurant with predictably exceptional wine list, **Osteria dell'Enoteca** (📞 055 21 27 04; www.osteriadellenoteca.com; Via Romana 70r; meals €30; 🕒 noon-2.30pm & 7-11pm Wed-Mon), nearby.

Dolce Vita
BAR

24 🚇 MAP P130, D3

Going strong since the 1980s, this cult bar with subtle club vibe is an

Drinking fountain, Oltrarno

ELENA ODAREEVA/SHUTTERSTOCK ©

Oltrarno hot spot for after-work drinks, cocktails and DJ sets. Its chic, design-driven interior gets a new look every month thanks to constantly changing photography and contemporary art exhibitions. Its summertime decked terrace is the place to be seen (shades obligatory). Live bands, too.

Food is available, including a gluten-free or English breakfast option (€7 to €9.50) and weekend brunch. (📞055 28 45 95; www.dolcevitafirenze.it; Piazza del Carmine 6r; 🕙9am-2am, closed 2 weeks Aug & Jan)

Archea Brewery

CRAFT BEER

25 🍺 MAP P130, D4

Craft-beer devotees will enjoy this dimly lit, hole-in-the-wall drinking joint, a step away from the tourist crowds with knowledgeable bartenders at the helm and locals firmly planted around the L-shaped bar. Pick from an interesting range of home and guest brews, bottled and on tap, from Italy and Europe. Four-beer tasting flights too. (www.facebook.com/archea.brwry; Via dei Serragli 44; 🕙6pm-1am Mon-Thu, to 2am Fri & Sat, 4.30pm-1am Sun)

Shopping

Obsequium

WINE

26 🔒 MAP P130, G4

Tuscan wines, wine accessories and gourmet foods, including truffles, in one of the city's finest wine shops – on the ground floor of one of Florence's best-preserved medieval towers to boot. Not sure which wine to buy? Linger over a glass or indulge in a three-wine tasting (from €15) and an accompanying *taglieri* (board) of mixed cheese and salami (€13).

The boutique also offers Tuscan olive oil and balsamic vinegar tastings (both €7). Reserve tastings in advance online. (📞055 21 68 49; www.obsequium.it; Borgo San Jacopo 17/39; 🕙11am-9pm Mon-Sat, from noon Sun)

Bjørk

FASHION & ACCESSORIES

27 🔒 MAP P130, G4

Cutting-edge fashion is what this trendy concept store, incongruously wedged between tatty old artisanal workshops on an Oltrarno backstreet, sells. It is the creation of well-travelled Florentine and fashionista Filippo Anzaione, whose taste in Italian and other contemporary European designers is impeccable. (📞333 9795839; www.facebook.com/bjorkflorence; Via della Sprone 25r; ⏱2.30-7.30pm Mon, 10.30am-1.30pm & 2.30-7.30pm Tue-Sat)

Reinhard Plank
FASHION & ACCESSORIES

28 🔒 MAP P130, D4

Exquisite hand-made hats crafted with extraordinary passion and creativity by Austrian-born, Florence-based designer Reinhard Plank is what this tiny boutique is about. Each hat, invariably casual and highly wearable, is utterly unique – in both shape and material. (📞388-7520833; www.reinhardplank.it; Via dei Serragli 36r; ⏱11am-1pm & 5.30-7.30pm Mon-Sat, variable Sun)

Avavav
FASHION & ACCESSORIES

29 🔒 MAP P130, F6

Affordable luxury and Tuscan craftsmanship are perfect companions at this sustainable-fashion boutique for women. Swedish couple Linda and Adam Friberg, at home in Florence, are the creative pair behind the fast-growing, elegant and functional label. Think slinky silky pantsuits, flowery flow-

Oltrarno Markets

Watch for an arts and crafts market on Piazza Santo Spirito on the second Sunday of each month, and an organic farmers market on the third Sunday. Most days, a handful of stalls selling fruit and veg pepper the lovely square.

ing frocks, vintage print scarves, a smattering of faux fur and the occasional recycled fabric from a top-end brand.

Ring the bell to enter. (www.avavav.com; Via Maggio 15; ⏱10am-6pm Mon-Fri, hours vary Sat & Sun)

Laboratorio Jane Harman
ARTS & CRAFTS

30 🔒 MAP P130, B2

Florence resident since the '80s, British-born Jane Harman is an antiques restorer with more than 30 years' experience. She's opened this quaint store by her south-of-the-river workshop selling contemporary items, all made of wood, from jewellery to mini versions of the local church of Santo Spirito. Her handmade pieces make unique souvenirs. (📞329 0704920; www.harmanjane.it; Via L Bartolini 1r; ⏱8am-12.30pm & 2-6pm Mon-Fri)

Explore ⊕
Pisa

Once a maritime power to rival Genoa and Venice, Pisa now draws its fame from an architectural project gone terribly wrong. But the world-famous Leaning Tower is just one of many noteworthy sights in this compact and compelling city. Romanesque buildings, Gothic churches and Renaissance piazzas abound, and there's also a vibrant and affordable cafe and bar scene.

The Short List

○ **Leaning Tower (p145)** *Scaling one of the world's most iconic towers at sunset to devour pink-hued views of grassy green Piazza dei Miracoli and its prized collection of marble monuments.*

○ **Camposanto (p146)** *Contemplating emotive frescoes in the peaceful cloisters of Pisa's monumental cemetery.*

○ **Palazzo Blu (p149)** *Catching a contemporary art exhibition at this riverside gallery showcasing modern Pisan art.*

○ **Gelateria De' Coltelli (p151)** *Exploding your taste-buds with gelato in a wild rainbow of flavours from Pisa's favourite ice-cream parlour.*

Getting There

🚃 Regular services leave Florence (€8.40, 1¼ hours) for Pisa Centrale station.

🚗 Take the toll-free SCG FI-PI-LI (SS67) from Florence. Street parking costs €2 per hour. Park outside the historic centre's Limited Traffic Zone (ZTL); find a free car park on Lungarno Guadalongo, south side of the Arno.

Pisa Map on p148

Piazza dei Miracoli (p144) AUM STUDIO/SHUTTERSTOCK ©

Top Experience 📷
Lean in at Piazza dei Miracoli

No Tuscan sight is more immortalised in kitsch souvenirs than the iconic tower teetering on the edge of this vast green square, also known as Piazza del Duomo (Cathedral Sq). Its lawns provide an urban carpet on which Europe's most extraordinary concentration of Romanesque buildings lounge: the duomo (cathedral), battistero (baptistry) and campanile (bell tower; aka the Leaning Tower).

◉ MAP P148, B1

Campo dei Miracoli

📞 050 83 50 11

www.opapisa.it

Leaning Tower

Yes, it's true: Pisa's famous **tower** (Torre Pendente; €18; 8.30am-10pm mid-Jun–Aug, 9am-8pm Apr–mid-Jun & Sep, to 7pm Oct & Mar, to 6pm Nov-Feb) really does lean. The steep climb up its 300-odd steps is strenuous and can be tricky (children under eight are not admitted; those aged eight to 12 years must hold an adult's hand), but the views from the top make it well worthwhile. Buy tickets from one of two well-signposted ticket offices: the main ticket office behind the tower or the smaller office inside Museo delle Sinopie (p146).

Duomo

Pisa's huge 11th-century **duomo** (Duomo di Santa Maria Assunta; admission free; 10am-8pm Apr-Oct, to 6pm or 7pm Nov-Feb), with its striking cladding of green and cream marble (a 13th-century addition), was the blueprint for Romanesque churches throughout Tuscany. The elliptical dome, the first of its kind in Europe at the time, dates from 1380 and the wooden ceiling decorated with 24-carat gold is a legacy of Medici rule.

Battistero

Construction of the cupcake-style **Battistero** (Battistero di San Giovanni; €5, combination ticket with Camposanto or Museo delle Sinopie €7, Camposanto & Museo delle Sinopie €8; 8am-8pm Apr-Oct, 9am-6pm or 7pm Nov-Mar) began in 1152, but the building was remodelled and continued by Nicola and Giovanni Pisano more than a century later and finally completed in the 14th century. Don't leave without climbing to the Upper Gallery to listen to the custodian demonstrate the double dome's remarkable acoustics and echo effects.

Inside the Battistero, a hexagonal marble pulpit (1260) by Nicola Pisano is the undoubted highlight. Inspired by the Roman sarcophagi in the Camposanto, Pisano used powerful classical models to enact scenes from biblical legend.

★ Top Tips

o There are limited admissions to the Leaning Tower: book in advance online or grab the first available slot as soon as you arrive.

o Admission to the *duomo* is free, but you need to show a ticket – either for one of the other sights or a *duomo* coupon distributed at ticket offices.

o For an alternative view of the square, get up on the **city walls** (050 098 74 80; www.muradipisa. it; Piazza del Duomo; adult/reduced €3/2; 9am-7pm Apr-Mat & Sep, 9am-7pm Mon-Thu, to 9pm Fri-Sun Jun-Aug, shorter hours rest of year;).

✕ Take a Break

Pick up a *cecina* (chickpea pizza) or a *focaccine* (small flat roll) from Pizzeria Il Montino (p150).

Break with coffee or a drink at historic Caffè Pasticceria Salza (p151).

His figure of Daniel, who supports one of the corners of the pulpit on his shoulders, is particularly extraordinary.

Camposanto

Soil shipped from Calvary during the Crusades is said to lie within the white walls of this hauntingly beautiful **cloistered quadrangle** (Piazza del Duomo; €5, combination ticket with Battistero or Museo delle Sinopie €7, Battistero & Museo €8; ⊙8am-8pm Apr-Jul, Sep & Oct, 8am-10pm Aug, 9am-7pm Nov, Dec & Mar, 9am-5pm Jan & Feb), where prominent Pisans were once buried. It's a peaceful sanctuary after the selfie mayhem on the square outside. Some of the sarcophagi here are of Graeco-Roman origin, recycled during the Middle Ages. During WWII, Allied artillery destroyed many of the 14th- and 15th-century frescoes that once covered the cloister walls. Those in the southern cloister have been beautifully restored.

Among the Camposanto's frescoes to survive were Buonamico Buffalmacco's remarkable illustrations of hell, painted between 1336 and 1341. In *Inferno* (second fresco to the right of main entrance) Lucifer dances in hell greedily devouring sinners and excreting them, while ape-like demons dance around him in torment. In *Triumph of Death* (fourth fresco on right) graphic imagery shows the damned being roasted alive on spits.

Museo delle Sinopie

Home to some fascinating frescoes, this **museum** (Piazza del Duomo;

Camposanto

Why It Leans

In 1160 Pisa boasted 10,000-odd towers, but no *campanile* (bell tower) for its cathedral. Loyal Pisan, Berta di Bernardo, righted this in 1172 when she died and left a legacy of 60 pieces of silver in her will to the city to get cracking on a *campanile*.

Ironically, when Bonnano Pisano set to work on the world's most famous *campanile* in 1173, he did not realise what shaky ground he was on: beneath Piazza dei Miracoli's lawns lay a treacherous mix of sand and clay, 40m deep. And when work stopped five years on, with just three storeys completed, Italy's stump of an icon already tilted. Building resumed in 1272, workers compensating for the lean by building straight up from the lower storeys to create a subtle banana curve. By the 19th century, many were convinced the tower was a mere whimsical folly of its inventors, built deliberately to lean.

In 1838 a clean-up job to remove muck oozing from the base of the tower exposed, once and for all, the true nature of its precarious foundations. In the 1950s the seven bells inside the tower, each sounding a different musical note and rung from the ground by 14 men since 1370, were silenced for fear of a catastrophic collapse. In 1990 the tower was closed to the public. Engineers placed 1000 tonnes of lead ingots on the north side to counteract the subsidence on the south side. Steel bands were wrapped around the 2nd storey to keep it together.

Then in 1995 the tower slipped a whole 2.5mm. Steel braces were slung around the 3rd storey of the tower and attached to heavy hydraulic A-frame anchors some way from the northern side. The frames were replaced by steel cables, attached to neighbouring buildings. The tower held in place, engineers gingerly removed 70 tonnes of earth from below the northern foundations, forcing the tower to sink to its 18th-century level – and correct the lean by 2011 to 43.8cm. Success...

Every year scientists carry out tests on Pisa's pearly white leaning tower to measure its lean and check that it's stable. Ironically, results in 2013 showed that the world's most famous leaning tower had, in fact, lost 2.5cm of its iconic lean, with some scientists even predicting a complete self-straightening by the year 2300. Let's hope not.

€5, combination ticket with Battistero or Camposanto €7, Battistero & Camposanto €8; ☻8am-8pm Apr-Nov, 9am-6pm or 7pm Nov-Feb) safeguards several *sinopie* (preliminary sketches) drawn by artists in red earth pigment on the walls of the Camposanto in the 14th and 15th centuries before frescoes were painted over them. It offers a compelling study in fresco painting technique, with short films and scale models filling in the gaps.

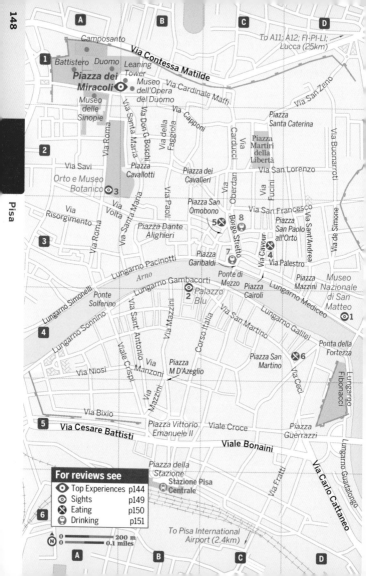

To A11; A12; FI-PI-LI;
Lucca (25km)

A

Camposanto

Via Contessa Matilde

1
Battistero   Duomo
Leaning
Tower

**Piazza dei
Miracoli** ◉

Museo
dell'Opera
del Duomo

Via Cardinale Maffi

Museo
delle
Sinopie

Via Santa Maria

Via Roma

Via Don G Boschi

Via della
Faggiola

Via Capponi

Via Carducci

Piazza
Santa Caterina

Via San Zeno

Via Buonarroti

2

Via Savi

Piazza
Cavallotti

Piazza dei
Cavalieri

Piazza
Martiri
della
Libertà

Via San Lorenzo

**Orto e Museo
Botanico** ◉ **3**

Via Volta

Via Santa Maria

Via Paoli

Via
Risorgimento

Via Roma

Piazza Dante
Alighieri

Piazza San
Omobono

Via Oberdan

Via Fucini

Via San Francesco

Via Sant'Andrea

Via di Simone

3

5 ✕

8 📍

Borgo Stretto

Piazza
San Paolo
all'Orto

4 📍 Via Palestro

Piazza
Garibaldi

7 📍

Via Cavour

Lungarno Pacinotti

Arno

Lungarno Gambacorti

Ponte di
Mezzo

Ponte di
Mezzo

Piazza
Cairoli

Piazza
Mazzini

**Museo
Nazionale
di San
Matteo**

Ponte
Solferino

Lungarno Simonelli

**Palazzo
Blu** ◉
2

Lungarno Mediceo

1 ◉

Lungarno Sonnino

Via Sant' Antonio

Via Mazzini

Corso Italia

Via San Martino

Lungarno Galilei

4

Via Niosi

Viale Crispi

Via
Manzoni

Piazza
M D'Azeglio

Via Mazzini

Piazza San
Martino

6 ✕

Ponta della
Fortezza

Via Ceci

Lungarno Fibonacci

Via Bixio

Piazza Vittorio
Emanuele II

Viale Croce

Piazza
Guerrazzi

5
Via Cesare Battisti

Viale Bonaini

Lungarno Guadalongo

Via Carlo Cattaneo

Piazza della
Stazione

🚉 Stazione Pisa
Centrale

Via Fratti

6

To Pisa International
Airport (2.4km)

For reviews see

◉	Top Experiences	p144
◉	Sights	p149
✕	Eating	p150
📍	Drinking	p151

Ⓝ 0 ————— 200 m
    0 ————— 0.1 miles

A   **B**   **C**   **D**

Sights

Museo Nazionale di San Matteo

MUSEUM

1 ◉ MAP P148, D4

This inspiring repository of medieval masterpieces sits in a 13th-century Benedictine convent on the Arno's northern waterfront boulevard. The museum's collection of paintings from the Tuscan school (c 12th to 14th centuries) is notable, with works by Lippo Memmi, Taddeo Gaddi, Gentile da Fabriano and Ghirlandaio. Don't miss Masaccio's *St Paul*, Fra' Angelico's *Madonna of Humility* and Simone Martini's *Polyptych of Saint Catherine*. (📞 050 54 18 65; Piazza San Matteo in Soarta 1; adult/

reduced €5/2.50; ⏱8.30am-7.30pm Tue-Sat, to 1.30pm Sun)

Palazzo Blu

GALLERY

2 ◉ MAP P148, B3

Facing the river is this magnificently restored 14th-century building with a striking dusty-blue facade. Inside, its over-the-top 19th-century interior decoration is the perfect backdrop for the Foundation Pisa's art collection – predominantly Pisan works from the 14th to 20th centuries on the 2nd floor. Admission includes an **archaeological area** in the basement and the noble **residence** of this aristocratic palace, furnished as it would have been in the 19th century, on the 1st floor.

Museo Nazionale di San Matteo

DIMA MOROZ/SHUTTERSTOCK ©

Keith Haring & Artburger ⌐⟫

Burger cafe **Artburger** (www.facebook.com/artburgerpisa; Via Zandonai 4; ⏱noon-3pm & 6-11pm; 📶) stares face to face with *Tuttomondo* (1989), the last wall mural American pop artist Keith Haring painted just months before his death on the facade of a Pisan church. Have a drink on the terrace and lament the fading, weather-beaten colours of Haring's 30 signature prancing dancing men.

Temporary exhibitions command a higher admission fee (€6/4). (📞050 220 46 50; www.palazzoblu.it; Lungarno Gambacorti 9; adult/reduced €3/2; ⏱10am-7pm Mon-Fri, to 8pm Sat & Sun, shorter hours winter)

Orto e Museo Botanico
GARDENS

3 ◎ MAP P148, A2

For a Zen-like respite from the Piazza dei Miracoli crowd, explore this peaceful walled garden laced with centurion palm trees, flora typical to the Apuane Alps, a fragrant herb garden, vintage greenhouses and 35 orchid species. Showcasing the botanical collection of Pisa University, the garden dates from 1543 and was Europe's first university botanical garden, tended by the illustrious

botanist Luca Ghini (1490–1556). The museum, inside **Palazzo della Conchiglie**, explores the garden's history, with exquisite botanical drawings, catalogues, maquettes etc. (Botanical Garden & Museum; 📞050 221 13 10; www.ortomuseobot.sma.unipi.it; Via Roma 56; adult/reduced €4/2; ⏱8.30am-8pm Apr-Sep, 9am-5pm Mon-Sat, to 1am Sun Oct-Mar)

Eating

Osteria Bernardo
TUSCAN €€

4 ✕ MAP P148, C3

This small bistro on a pretty square, well away from the Leaning Tower crowd, is the perfect fusion of easy dining and gourmet excellence. Its menu is small – just four or five dishes per course – and the cuisine is creative. Think pistachio-crusted lamb, beef in beer sauce or a tasty risotto with Stilton cheese, lettuce and crisp leek. Reservations recommended. (by Il Giardino Nascosto; 📞050 57 52 16; www.facebook.com/osteriabernardoby giardinonascosto; Piazza San Paolo all'Orto 1; meals €40; ⏱12.30-3pm & 7-11pm Tue-Sun)

Pizzeria Il Montino
PIZZA €

5 ✕ MAP P148, C3

There's nothing fancy about this down-to-earth pizzeria, an icon among Pisans, students and sophisticates alike. Take away or order at the bar then grab a table, inside or out, and munch on house specialities such as *cecina* (chickpea pizza), *castagnaccio* (chestnut cake) and *spuma* (sweet, nonalcoholic drink). Or go for a *focaccine* (small flat roll) filled with salami, pancetta or *porchetta* (suckling pig). (☎050 59 86 95; Vicolo del Monte 1; pizza €6-8.50, foccacine €2.50-5, cecina €2; ⊙11am-3pm & 5.30-10.30pm Mon-Sat)

Ristorante Galileo   TUSCAN €€

6 ✖ MAP P148, D4

For good, honest, unpretentious Tuscan cooking, nothing beats this classical old-timer. From the cork-covered wine list to the complimentary plate of warm homemade focaccia and huge platters of tempting *cantuccini* (almond-studded biscuits), Galileo makes you feel welcome. Fresh pasta is strictly hand- and homemade, and most veggies are plucked fresh that morning from the restaurant's garden. (☎050 2 82 87; www.ristorantegalileo.com; Via San Martino 6-8; meals €25-35; ⊙12.30-2.30pm & 7.30-11pm)

Drinking

Bazeel   BAR

7 🍸 MAP P148, C3

A dedicated all-rounder, Bazeel is a hotspot from dawn to dark. Laze over breakfast, linger over a pizza or hang out with the A-list crowd over a generous *aperitivo* spread, live music and DJs. Its chapel-like interior is nothing short of fabulous, as is its pavement terrace out

the front. Check its Facebook feed for what's on. (☎349 0880688; www.bazeel.it; Lungarno Pacinotti 1; ⊙7am-1am Sun-Thu, to 2am Fri & Sat)

Caffè Pasticceria Salza   CAFE

8 🍸 MAP P148, C3

This old-fashioned cake shop has been tempting Pisans into sugar-induced wickedness since 1898. It's an equally lovely spot for a cocktail – any time. Check its Facebook page for enticing foodie events and happenings. (☎050 58 01 44; Borgo Stretto 44; ⊙8am-8.30pm Tue-Sun)

The Best Gelati

Follow the crowd to world-class **Gelateria De' Coltelli** (☎345 4811903; www.decoltelli.it; Lungarno Pacinotti 23; small/medium/large €2.50/3/4.30; ⊙11.30am-10.30pm Sun-Thu, to 11.30pm Fri & Sat), famed for its sensational artisanal, organic and 100% natural gelato. Flavours are as zesty and appealing as its bright-orange interior. The hard part is choosing: ginger, ricotta cheese with pine nuts and honey, candied chestnuts, almond with candied lemon peel, cashew with Maldon salt, kiwi, or ricotta with candied orange peel and chocolate chips.

Worth a Trip 👀
Lucca

Lovely Lucca endears itself to everyone who visits. Hidden behind imposing Renaissance walls, its cobbled streets, handsome piazzas, Romaneqsue churches and shady promenades make it a perfect destination to explore by foot. Its laid-back, alfresco cafe life is perfect for relaxing over a coffee or glass of Lucchesi wine and a slow progression of rustic dishes prepared with fresh produce from the surrounding countryside.

🚆 **Train** From Florence (€7.50 to €9.60, 1¼ to 1¾ hours, hourly).

🚗 **Car** A11 from Florence. Park in Parcheggio Carducci nearPorta Sant'Anna.

Tourist office (☎0583 58 31 50; www.turismo. lucca.it; Piazzale Verdi; ◷9.30am-6.30pm)

City Walls

Lucca's monumental *mura* (wall; 12m high, 4km long) was built around the old city in the 16th and 17th centuries. Its ramparts are crowned with a tree-lined footpath – a local favourite for a bike ride, picnic and sacrosanct *passeggiata*. **Biciclette Poli** and **Cicli Bizzarri** on Piazza Santa Maria hire bikes (per hour/day €3/15; 9am to 7pm summer).

Cattedrale di San Martino

This predominantly Romanesque **cathedral** (pictured; ☎0583 49 05 30; www.museocattedralelucca.it; Piazza San Martino; €3, incl campanile, Museo della Cattedrale & Chiesa e Battistero dei SS Giovanni & Reparata adult/reduced €9/6; ☺9.30am-6.30pm Mon-Fri, to 6.45pm Sat, noon-6.30pm Sun) dates to the start of the 11th century. Inside, the **Volto Santo** is a simply fashioned Christ on a wooden crucifix that dates from the 13th century.

Torre Guinigi

The bird's-eye view from the top of this medieval, 45m-tall red-brick tower is magnificent – as are the seven oak trees planted in a U-shaped flower bed at the top. Count 230 steps up.

Palazzo Pfanner

Take a stroll around this beautiful, 17th-century **palace** (☎0583 95 21 55; www.palazzopfanner. it; Via degli Asili 33; palace or garden adult/reduced €4.50/4, both €6.50/5.50; ☺10am-6pm Apr-Nov) where parts of Jane Campion's *The Portrait of a Lady* (1996) were shot. Highlights include the frescoed, furnished *piano nobile* (main reception room) and the enchanting baroque-styled garden with ornamental pond, lemon house and 18th-century statues of Greek gods posing between potted lemon trees.

★ **Top Tips**

○ Stroll boutique-filled **Via Fillungo**; duck down a side street off its northeastern end to uncover oval-shaped **Piazza dell'Anfiteatro**, named after an amphitheatre located here in Roman times.

✕ **Take a Break**

○ For picnic provisions, go to **Forno Amedeo Giusti** (☎0583 49 62 85; www.facebook.com/PanificioGiusti; Via Santa Lucia 20; pizzas & filled focaccias per kg €10-15; ☺7am-7.30pm Mon-Sat, to 1.30pm Sun) for fresh-from-the-oven pizza and *focaccia* or **Da Felice** (☎0583 49 49 86; www.pizzeriadafelice. it; Via Buia 12; focaccia & pizza slices €1-5; ☺11am-8.30pm Mon, 10am-8.30pm Tue-Sat) for *cecina* (salted chickpea pizza) and *castagnacci* (chestnut cakes).

Explore ◈

Siena

Unesco includes Siena's centro storico (historical centre) in its famed World Heritage list, citing it as the living embodiment of a medieval city. Easily explored in a day, the glories of its Gothic architecture and art provide a fascinating contrast to the Renaissance splendour that is so evident in Florence, making it a compelling side trip.

The Short List

○ **Duomo (p156)** *Getting lost in the cathedral's mesmerising treasury of exquisite floor panels, library books, frescoes, sculptures and more.*

○ **Porta del Cielo (p159)** *Devouring spectacular aerial views of the cathedral interior and exterior from its rooftop and dome.*

○ **Museo Civico (p161)** *Getting to grips with Sienese fresco artistry inside the city museum.*

○ **Piazza del Campo (p161)** *Enjoying an alfresco coffee or aperitivo on Siena's central square.*

○ **Palio (p166)** *Joining in the fun, games and merriment surrounding Siena's famous annual horse race.*

Getting There

🚌 Frequent express buses leave from Florence's SITA bus station (€7.80, 1¼ hours).

🚗 Florence–Siena speedy S2 or more scenic SR222. Park (€1.70 per hour) in car parks at San Francesco, Stadio Comunale, Fortezza Medicea and Santa Caterina.

Siena Map on p160

Palio (p166) M. ROHANA/SHUTTERSTOCK ©

Top Experience 📷

Marvel at the Opera della Metropolitana di Siena

Siena's Gothic duomo (Cattedrale di Santa Maria Assunta) is the focal point of an ecclesiastical complex that includes a museum, baptistry and crypt. All are embellished with wonderful art – Giovanni and Nicola Pisano, Pinturicchio, Jacopo della Quercia, Ghiberti, Donatello and Duccio di Buoninsegna are among the artists whose works glorified their city and their god.

◉ MAP P160, A4

📞 0577 28 63 00

www.operaduomo.siena.it

Mar-Oct €5, Nov-Feb free, when floor displayed €8

🕑 10.30am-7pm Mon-Sat, 1.30-6pm Sun Mar-Oct, 10.30am-5.30pm Mon-Sat, 1.30-5.30pm Sun Nov-Feb

Duomo

Construction of the *duomo* started in the 12th century and work continued well into the 14th century. The magnificent facade of white, green and red marble was designed by Giovanni Pisano; the statues of philosophers and prophets are copies; you'll find the originals in the Museo dell'Opera (p158). The interior is truly stunning, with walls and pillars continuing the black-and-white-stripe theme of the exterior.

Libreria Piccolomini

Through a door from the north aisle of the *duomo* is this enchanting **library**, built to house the books of Enea Silvio Piccolomini, better known as Pope Pius II. Its walls are decorated with richly detailed frescoes painted between 1503 and 1508 by Bernardino (di Betto) Pinturicchio and depicting events in the life of Piccolomini, including his ordination as pope.

Pisano's Pulpit

The *duomo's* exquisitely crafted marble-and-porphyry pulpit was created between 1265 and 1268 by Nicola Pisano, who had previously carved the famed pulpit in Pisa's *duomo*. Assisted by his son Giovanni and assistant Arnolfo di Cambio, Pisano depicted powerful scenes including the Last Judgement.

The Floor Panels

The inlaid-marble floor, decorated with 56 panels by about 40 artists and executed from the 14th to the 19th centuries, depicts historical and biblical subjects. About half of the panels are obscured by protective covering, and are revealed only between mid-August and late October each year (an extra fee applies).

★ Top Tips

o You'll save money by purchasing a combined OPA SI or Acropoli Pass, valid for three days, rather than individual tickets.

o Walking tours offered by **Centro Guide Turistiche Siena e Provincia** (📞0577 4 32 73; www.guidesiena.it) and **Associazione Centro Guide** (AGT; 📞0577 4 32 73; www.guidesiena.it/en) include a tour of the *duomo*.

✕ Take a Break

Nearby La Vecchia Latteria (p167) serves the best gelato in the city.

Stop by Il Magnifico (p169) to pick up some almond biscuits to fuel your museum wandering.

Battistero di San Giovanni

Behind the *duomo*, down a steep flight of steps, is the frescoed **baptistry** (Piazza San Giovanni; adult/child €6/1; ⏰10.30am-6.30pm Mon-Sat & 1.30-5.30pm Sun Mar-Oct, 10.30am-5pm Mon-Sat & 1.30-5pm Sun Nov-Feb). At its centre is a hexagonal marble font (c 1417) by Jacopo della Quercia, decorated with bronze panels depicting the life of St John the Baptist by artists including Lorenzo Ghiberti (*Baptism of Christ* and *St John in Prison;* 1427) and Donatello (*The Head of John the Baptist Being Presented to Herod;* 1427).

Cripta

This **space** (Piazza San Giovanni; adult/child €6/1; ⏰10.30am-6.30pm Mon-Sat & 1.30-5.30pm Sun Mar-Oct, 10.30am-5pm Mon-Sat & 1.30-5pm Sun Nov-Feb)

beneath the cathedral's pulpit was rediscovered and restored in 1999 after having been filled to the roof with debris in the 1300s. The walls are completely covered with *pintura a secco* ('dry painting', better known as 'mural painting') dating back to the 1200s. There are some 180 sq metres worth, depicting biblical stories, including the Passion of Jesus and the Crucifixion.

Museo dell'Opera

The collection in this **museum** (Piazza Duomo; adult/child €6/1; ⏰10.30am-6.30pm Mon-Sat & 1.30-5.30pm Sun Mar–mid-Apr, from 10am mid-Apr–Oct, 10.30am-5pm Mon-Sat & 1.30-5pm Sun Nov-Feb) showcases artworks that formerly adorned the *duomo*, including the 12 statues of prophets and philosophers (1285–87) by

Fresco in Libreria Piccolomini (p157)

Giovanni Pisano that decorated its facade. Pisano designed these to be viewed from ground level, which is why they look so distorted as they crane uncomfortably forward. Also notable is the vibrant stained-glass window designed and painted by Duccio di Buoninsegna (1287–90).

Duccio's Maestà

Taking centre stage in the Museo dell'Opera del Duomo's collection is Duccio di Buoninsegna's striking *Maestà* (1308–11), which was painted on both sides as a screen for the *duomo's* high altar. The main painting portrays the Virgin surrounded by angels and saints; the rear panels (sadly incomplete) portray 26 scenes from the Passion of Christ.

Panorama del Facciatone

In 1339 the city's leaders decided to transform the cathedral into one of Italy's biggest churches, but the plague of 1348 scotched their plan to build an immense new nave with the present church as the transept. Known as the Duomo Nuovo (New Cathedral), all that remains of the project is this **panoramic terrace** (Piazza Duomo; ⏲10.30am-6.30pm Mon-Sat & 1.30-5.30pm Sun Mar–mid-Apr, from 10am Mon-Sat mid-Apr–Oct, 10.30am-5pm Mon-Sat & 1.30-5pm Sun Nov-Feb), accessed through the museum.

Pius II

Born Enea Silvio Piccolomini in the village of Corsignano (now Pienza) south of Siena, Pope Pius II (1405–64) was a tireless traveller, noted humanist, talented diplomat, exhaustive autobiographer (13 volumes!) and medieval urban-planning trendsetter. Also a scholar, poet and writer of erotic and comic stories, Pius built a huge personal library that was relocated to the purpose-built Libreria Piccolomini (p157) in Siena's *duomo* after his death by order of his nephew, Cardinal Francesco Todeschini Piccolomini, the future pope Pius III.

Porta del Cielo

To enjoy spectacular bird's-eye views of the interior and exterior of Siena's cathedral, buy a ticket for the **Gate of Heaven** (adult/child €20/5; ⏲10.30am-7pm Mon-Sat, 1.30-5.30pm Sun Mar-late Aug & late Oct-early Jan, 10.30am-7pm Mon-Sat, 9.30am-5.30pm Sun late Aug-late Oct) escorted tour up, into and around the building's roof and dome. Tour groups are capped at 18 participants and depart at fixed times throughout the day – purchase your ticket from the office in Santa Maria della Scala. Note that you'll need to arrive at the meeting point at least five minutes before your allocated tour time.

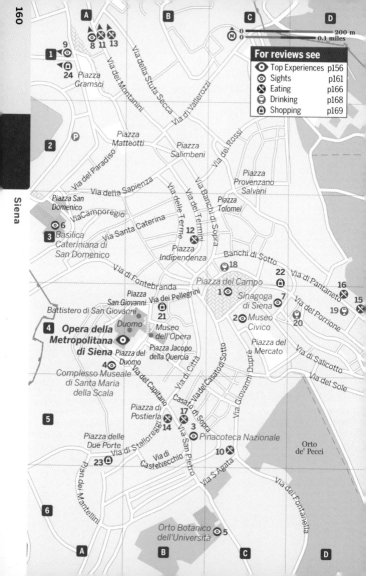

For reviews see

	Top Experiences	p156
	Sights	p161
	Eating	p166
	Drinking	p168
	Shopping	p169

A

9
1
24 *Piazza Gramsci*

8 11 13

Via della Stufa Secca

Via dei Montanini

B

Via di Vallerozzi

C

N
0 — 200 m
0 — 0.1 miles

D

2

Piazza Matteotti

Piazza Salimbeni

Via del Paradiso

Via della Sapienza

Via dei Rossi

Piazza Provenzano Salvani

Piazza San Domenico

Via Camporegio

Via Santa Caterina

Via delle Terme

Via dei Banchi di Sopra

Via dei Termini

Piazza Tolomei

6
3 *Basilica Cateriniana di San Domenico*

12

Piazza Indipendenza

Banchi di Sotto

22

Via di Pantaneto

16

Via di Fontebranda

Via del Pellegrini

18
Piazza del Campo

1

Sinagoga di Siena

7

15

19
20

Via del Porrione

Piazza San Giovanni

21

Battistero di San Giovanni

Museo dell'Opera

Duomo

2
Museo Civico

4 **Opera della Metropolitana di Siena**

4

Piazza del Duomo

Piazza Jacopo della Quercia

Piazza del Mercato

Complesso Museale di Santa Maria della Scala

Via del Capitano

Via di Città

Via di Casato di Sotto

Casato di Sopra

Via Giovanni Dupré

Via di Salicotto

Via del Sole

5

Piazza di Postierla

17
14

3

Pinacoteca Nazionale

Orto de' Pecci

Piazza delle Due Porte

Via di Stalloreggi

Via San Pietro

10

Via di Salicotto

23

Via di Castelvecchio

Via S. Agata

Via del Fontanella

6

Prau dei Mantellini

Orto Botanico dell'Università

5

A   **B**   **C**   **D**

Sights

Piazza del Campo

PIAZZA

1  MAP P160, C4

Popularly known as 'Il Campo', this sloping piazza has been Siena's social centre since being staked out by the ruling Consiglio dei Nove (Council of Nine) in the mid-12th century. Built on the site of a Roman marketplace, its paving is divided into nine sectors representing the members of the *consiglio,* and these days acts as a carpet on which young locals meet and relax. The cafes around its perimeter are the most popular coffee and *aperitivo* spots in town.

Museo Civico

MUSEUM

2  MAP P160, C4

Entered via the Palazzo Pubblico's **Cortile del Podestà** (Courtyard of the Chief Magistrate), this wonderful museum showcases rooms richly frescoed by artists of the Sienese school. Commissioned by the city's governing body rather than by the Church, some of the frescoes depict secular subjects – highly unusual at the time. The highlights are two huge frescoes: Ambrogio Lorenzetti's *Allegories of Good and Bad Government* (c 1338–40) and Simone Martini's celebrated *Maestà* (*Virgin Mary in Majesty;* 1315). (Civic Museum; 0577 29 26 15; Palazzo Pubblico, Piazza del Campo 1; adult/reduced €10/9, with Torre del Mangia €15,

Piazza del Campo

MILA ATKOVSKA/SHUTTERSTOCK ©

with Torre del Mangia & Complesso Museale di Santa Maria della Scala

€20; ⏱10am-6.15pm mid-Mar–Oct, to 5.15pm Nov–mid-Mar)

Inside the Museo Civico

After purchasing your ticket, head upstairs to the **Sala del Risorgimento**, where late-19th-century frescoes serialise key events in the Risorgimento (reunification period). Continue through to the **Sala di Balia** (Rooms of Authority), where frescoes by father-and-son Spinello and Parri Aretino recount episodes in the life of Pope Alexander III (the Sienese Rolando Bandinelli), including his clashes with the Holy Roman Emperor Frederick Barbarossa. Straight ahead is the **Sala del Concistoro** (Hall of the Council of Clergymen), dominated by the allegorical ceiling frescoes (1529–35) by the mannerist painter Domenico (di Pace) Beccafumi.

Through a vestibule to the left is the **Anticappella** (Chapel Entrance Hall) with frescoes painted in 1415 by Taddeo di Bartolo. These include figures representing the virtues needed for the proper exercise of power (Justice, Magnanimity, Strength, Prudence, Religion), and depictions of some of the leading Republican lights of ancient Rome. The **Cappella** (Chapel) contains a fine wooden choir and a fresco of the *Holy Family and St Leonard* by Il Sodoma, while the star attraction in the **Vestibolo** (Vestibule) is a bronze wolf, the symbol of Siena.

The vestibule leads into the **Sala del Mappamondo** (Hall of the World Map), which houses Simone Martini's powerful and striking *Maestà*, painted when he was only 21 years old. On the other side of the room is Martini's oft-reproduced fresco (1328–30) of Guidoriccio da Fogliano, a captain of the Sienese army.

The next room, the **Sala dei Nove** (Hall of the Nine), is where the ruling Council of Nine once met. It's decorated with Ambrogio Lorenzetti's fascinating fresco cycle, the *Allegories of Good and Bad Government* (c 1338–40). The central allegory portrays scenes with personifications of Justice, Wisdom, Virtue and Peace, all unusually depicted as women, along with scenes of criminal punishment and rewards for righteousness. Set perpendicular from it are the frescoes *Allegory of Good Government* and *Allegory of Bad Government*, which feature intensely contrasting scenes clearly set around Siena. The good depicts a sunlit, idyllic, serene city, with joyous citizens and a countryside filled with crops; the bad city is filled with vices, crime and disease.

Pinacoteca Nazionale   GALLERY

3 ⊙ MAP P160, B5

Siena's renovated art gallery, housed in 14th-century **Palazzo Buonsignori** since 1932, is home to an extraordinary collection of Gothic masterpieces from the Sienese school. These include works by Guido da Siena, Duccio (di Buoninsegna), Simone Martini, Niccolò di Segna, Lippo Memmi, Ambrogio and Pietro Lorenzetti, Bartolo di Fredi, Taddeo di Bartolo and Sano di Pietro. (📞0577 28 11 61; http://pinacotecanazionale.siena.it; Via San Pietro 29; adult/reduced €8/2; 🕑8.30am-1.30pm Fri-Mon, 2-7pm Tue-Thu, closed 2nd and 4th Sun of the month)

Complesso Museale di Santa Maria della Scala   MUSEUM

4 ⊙ MAP P160, A4

Built as a hospice for pilgrims travelling the Via Francigena, this huge complex opposite the *duomo* dates from the 13th century. Its highlight is the upstairs **Pellegrinaio** (Pilgrim's Hall), featuring vivid 15th-century frescoes by Lorenzo di Pietro (aka Vecchietta), Priamo della Quercia and Domenico di Bartolo. All laud the good works of the hospital and its patrons; the most evocative is di Bartolo's *Il governo degli infermi* (Caring for the Sick; 1440–41), which depicts many activities that occurred here. (📞0577 28 63 00; www.santamariadellascala.com;

Bird's-Eye City View

On Siena's central square, scale the graceful **Torre del Mangia** (📞0577 29 26 15; ticket@comune.siena.it; Palazzo Pubblico, Piazza del Campo 1; adult/family €10/25; 🕑10am-6.15pm Mar–mid-Oct, to 3.15pm mid-Oct–Feb) for killer bird's-eye views of the city laid out at your feet. Completed in 1348, this 87m-high red-brick-and-travertine bell tower is called the Tower of Eater after Giovanni di Balduccio, nicknamed 'Mangiaguadagni' ('Eat the Earnings'), who was employed by the municipality to beat the hours on its bell from 1347 to 1360.

Piazza Duomo 2; adult/reduced €9/7; 🕑10am-7pm Fri-Wed, to 10pm Thu mid-Mar–mid-Oct, to 5pm Mon, Wed & Fri, to 8pm Thu, to 7pm Sat & Sun mid-Oct–mid-Mar)

Orto Botanico dell'Università   GARDENS

5 ⊙ MAP P160, C6

The tranquil terraces of this botanical garden (1856), which is spread over 2.5 hectares of the verdant Sant'Agostino Valley, provide gorgeous views across the valley and a welcome escape from the tourist crowds. Owned by the University of Siena, which operates it as a centre for research and

Flee the Crowds

When the tourist crowd gets too much, retire to the tranquil terraces, tropical hothouses, fruit orchards and aromatic medicinal-plant gardens of Siena's **Orto Botanico** (p163). Spread over 2.5 hectares of the verdant Sant'Agostino Valley, the botanical gardens proffer gorgeous view across the valley.

Or explore **Orto de' Pecci** (📞0577 22 22 01; www.ortodepecci.it; Via Porta Giustizia; admission free; ⏰8.30am-10pm summer, reduced hr winter; 👶), an urban oasis with a small vineyard, an organic farm that supplies the on-site **restaurant** (pizza €6-9, meals €22; ⏰noon-2.30pm & 7.30-10pm Tue-Sun) with fruit and vegetables, plenty of animals (geese, goats, ducks and donkeys) and a scattering of site-specific contemporary artworks.

education, it features three greenhouses filled with tropical and subtropical species, a citrus house and gardens planted with ornamental, medicinal and food plants. Native and endangered species are also represented. (Botanical Garden of the University; 📞0577 23 20 76; www.simus.unisi.it/musei/mb; Via Pier Andrea Mattioli 4; adult/reduced

€5/2.50; ⏰10am-7pm Jul-Sep, to 5pm Mar-Jun, to 4pm Oct-Feb)

Basilica Cateriniana di San Domenico   CHURCH

6 ⊙ MAP P160, A3

St Catherine was welcomed into the Dominican fold within this huge and austere 13th-century basilica. Inside, the **Cappella di Santa Caterina** (halfway down the wall to the right of the altar) contains frescoes by Giovanni Antonio Bazzi (aka Il Sodoma) and Andrea Vanni depicting events in the saint's life. Also here are 15th-century reliquaries containing Catherine's head and one of her fingers, as well as a nastylooking chain that she is said to have flagellated herself with. (www.basilicacateriniana.com; Piazza San Domenico; admission free; ⏰7am-6.30pm Mar-Oct, 9am-6pm Nov-Feb)

Sinagoga di Siena   SYNAGOGUE

7 ⊙ MAP P160, C4

Sheltering behind an anonymous facade, this Ashkenazi synagogue in Siena's former Ghetto once serviced a community of 500. Sadly, a mere 50 Jews now live in the city. Functioning since 1731, the synagogue's rococo-style interior with its distinctive green-and-white colour scheme resembles an ornate church and can be visited on an enjoyable guided tour in which the history of the building and of Jews in Siena is recounted. Tours depart every 30 minutes. (Museo Ebraico di

Siena; 📳0577 27 13 45; www.jewish tuscany.it; Viccolo delle Scotte; adult/reduced €4/3; 🕙10.45am-4.45pm Sun, Mon & Thu)

Museo dell'Acqua   MUSEUM

8 🎯 MAP P160, A1

Siena is unusual in that unlike many Tuscan cities, it isn't located next to a watercourse. To compensate, it has a unique historical network of underground aqueducts known as *bottini*. This ingenious 25km system of excavated tunnels carries rainwater from the slopes of Mt Amiata to properties and above-ground fountains across the historical city and was in daily use until 1914. This multimedia museum above the Fonti di Pescaia celebrates this extraordinary engineering achievement. (📳0577

29 26 14, 0577 29 26 15; http://museo acqua.comune.siena.it; Strada delle Fonti di Pescaia 1; €10; 🕙10am-12.30pm & 4.30-7pm Thu-Sun Jun-Sep, 10am-noon Mon, Wed & Fri, 9.30am-12.30pm & 3-7pm Sat & Sun Oct-May)

Fortezza Medicea   CASTLE

9 🎯 MAP P160, A1

Built by order of Cosimo de' Medici in 1563, this fortified brick castle was decommissioned as a military barracks in the late 18th century and converted into a public park. It's now a popular leisure facility where locals come to relax in the garden or jog around the perimeter. There are panoramic city views from the ramparts and bastions. (Piazza Caduti delle Forze Armate; admission free; 🕙24hr)

Alley leading to Sinagoga di Siena

Eating

Osteria La Taverna di San Giuseppe

TUSCAN €€€

10 🗙 MAP P160, C5

Any restaurant specialising in beef, truffles and porcini mushrooms attracts our immediate attention, but not all deliver on their promise. Fortunately, this one does. A favoured venue for locals celebrating important occasions, it offers excellent food, an impressive wine list with plenty of local, regional and international choices, a convivial traditional atmosphere and efficient service. (📞0577 4 22 86; www.tavernasangiuseppe.it; Via Dupré 132; meals €49; ⊗noon-2.30pm & 7-10pm Mon-Sat)

Ristorante Enzo

TUSCAN €€€

11 🗙 MAP P160, A1

The epitome of refined Sienese dining, Da Enzo, as it is popularly called, welcomes guests with a complimentary glass of prosecco and follows up with Tuscan dishes made with skill and care. There's plenty of fish on the menu, as well as excellent handmade pasta and nonstandard meat dishes. The setting is equally impressive, with quality napery and glassware. (📞0577 28 12 77; www.daenzo.net; Via Camollia 49; meals €52; ⊗noon-2.30pm & 7.30-10pm Tue-Sun)

Festival in Siena: The Palio

Dating from the Middle Ages, this spectacular annual event includes a series of colourful pageants and a wild horse race on 2 July and 16 August in which 10 of Siena's 17 *contrade* (town districts) compete for the coveted *palio* (silk banner).

The race is staged in the Campo. From about 5pm, representatives from each *contrada* parade in historical costume, all bearing their individual banners. For scarcely one exhilarating minute, the 10 horses and their bareback riders tear three times around a temporarily constructed dirt racetrack with a speed and violence that makes spectators' hair stand on end.

The race is held at 7.45pm in July and 7pm in August. Join the crowds in the centre of the Campo at least four hours before the start if you want a place on the rails. Alternatively, cafes in the Campo sell expensive places on their terraces; these can be booked through the **tourist office** (📞0577 28 05 51; www.terresiena.it; Piazza Duomo 2, Santa Maria della Scala; ⊗10am-6pm mid-Mar–Oct, to 4.30pm Nov–mid-Mar) up to one year in advance.

Enoteca I Terzi
TUSCAN €€

12 ✖ MAP P160, B3

Close to the Campo but off the well-beaten tourist trail, this *enoteca* is located in a vaulted medieval building but has a contemporary feel. It's popular with sophisticated locals, who linger over working lunches, *aperitivo* sessions and slow-paced dinners featuring Tuscan *salumi* (cured meats), delicate handmade pasta, grilled meats and wonderful wines (many available by the glass). (☏0577 4 43 29; www.enotecaiterzi.it; Via dei Termini 7; meals €42; ☉12.30-3pm & 7.30-11pm Mon-Sat)

Osteria Il Vinaio
TUSCAN €

13 ✖ MAP P160, A1

Wine bars are thin on the ground here in Siena, so it's not surprising that Bobbe and Davide's neighbourhood *osteria* is so popular. Join the multigenerational local regulars for a bowl of pasta or your choice from the generous antipasto display, washed down with a glass or two of eminently quaffable house wine. (☏0577 4 96 15; Via Camollia 167; dishes €6.50-13; ☉10am-10pm Mon-Sat)

La Vecchia Latteria
GELATO €

14 ✖ MAP P160, B5

Sauntering through Siena's historic centre is always more fun with a gelato in hand. Just ask one of the many locals who are regular

Lunch Tip: La Prosciutteria 🍽

Buy a prosciutto-stuffed *panini* to go from La Prosciutteria and head to the Orto de' Pecci for a garden picnic.

customers at this *gelateria artigianale* (maker of handmade gelato) near the Pinacoteca Nazionale. Using quality produce, owners Fabio and Francesco concoct and serve fruity fresh or decadently creamy iced treats – choose from gelato or frozen yoghurt. (☏0577 05 76 38; www.facebook.com/Gelateria YogurteriaLaVecchiaLatteria; Via San Pietro 10; gelato €2-4.50; ☉noon-11pm, to 8pm winter)

La Prosciutteria
SANDWICHES €

15 ✖ MAP P160, D4

The name says it all. Prosciutto is the focus here, served in *panini* or on a *taglieri* (tasting board); cheese is an optional extra. Order to take away – the Orto de' Pecci (p164) is close by – or claim one of the tables on the street and enjoy a glass of wine (€2.50) too. An *aperitivo* (drink with snacks) costs €5. (☏0328 541 43 25; www.laprosciutteria.com; cnr Via Pantaneto & Vicolo Magalotti; panini €4-7; tasting boards from €10; ☉11.30am-3.30pm & 5.30pm-midnight Mon-Thu, 11.30am-12.30am Sat; 🛜)

Lievito M@dre

BAKERY €

16 ✕ MAP P160, D4

Close to the Campo, this popular bakery and cafe offers filled *panini* and slices of pizza to take away, as well as pizzas and cheap meal deals to enjoy at one of the inside tables. (📞0577 151 54 51; www.facebook.com/LievitoMadreSiena; Via di Pantaneto 59; meal deal €6.90, pizzas €6-12; ⏰7.30am-11pm Sun-Thu, to midnight Fi & Sat; 📶✏️)

Osteria Boccon del Prete

ITALIAN €€

17 ✕ MAP P160, B5

As popular with locals as it is with tourists, this casual place near the Pinacoteca Nazionale serves Tuscan dishes with a modern twist. The interior features a rich red

Panforte

ROMAN BABAKIN/SHUTTERSTOCK ©

colour scheme and modern art – very different to most of the city's eateries. (📞0577 28 03 88; www.facebook.com/boccondelpretesiena; Via San Pietro 17; meals €26; ⏰12.15-3pm & 7.15-10pm Mon-Sat)

Drinking

Bar Il Palio

CAFE

18 🍷 MAP P160, C3

Arguably the best coffee on the Campo; drink it standing at the bar or suffer the financial consequences. Service on the terrace, which is a popular *aperitivo* spot, can be excruciatingly slow. (📞0577 28 20 55; Piazza del Campo 47; ⏰8am-10pm, later in summer)

Bottega Roots

BAR

19 🍷 MAP P160, D4

Located in Siena's student quarter, this bar stages live-music acts in a vaulted interior with a mezzanine area. Artisan beer is the tipple of choice. Check its Facebook page for the performance schedule. (📞0577 89 24 82; www.facebook.com/bottegarootssiena; Via di Pantaneto 58; ⏰10.30am-2am; 📶)

UnTUBO

CLUB

20 🍷 MAP P160, D4

Live jazz acts regularly take the stage on Thursday and Friday nights at this intimate club near the Campo, which is popular with students and the city's boho set. Check the website for a full events program – blues, pop and rock acts drop in for occasional gigs too. Note that winter hours are often reduced. (📞0577 27 13 12; www.untubo.it; Vicolo del Luparello 2; cover charge varies; ⏰6.30pm-3am Tue-Sat)

Shopping

Il Magnifico FOOD

21 🅐 MAP P160, B4

Lorenzo Rossi is Siena's best baker, and his *panforte* (spiced fruit-and-nut cake), *ricciarelli* (sugar-dusted chewy almond biscuits) and *cavallucci* (chewy biscuits flavoured with aniseed and other spices) are a weekly purchase for most local households. Try them at his bakery and shop behind the *duomo*, and you'll understand why. (📞0577 28 11 06; www.ilmagnifico.siena.it; Via dei Pellegrini 27; ⏰7.30am-7.30pm Mon-Sat)

Aloe & Wolf VINTAGE

22 🅐 MAP P160, C3

Yearn to own labels such as Fendi, Gucci and Prada, but don't have the cash? This vintage shop just off the Campo may have the answer. Chock-full of Italian designer ensembles from the 1950s to recent times, it also stocks handbags, Borsalino hats and costume jewellery. (📞392 1819681; www.aloewolf.it; Via del Porrione 23; ⏰11am-7.30pm)

Campo Bar Chat

Via Camollia and Via di Pantaneto are Siena's major bar and coffee strips. Though atmospheric, the bars lining the Campo (p161) are expensive if you sit at a table – consider yourself warned.

Bottega d'Arte ART

23 🅐 MAP P160, A5

Inspired by the works of Sienese masters of the 14th and 15th centuries, artists Chiara Perinetti Casoni, Paolo Perinetti Casoni and Michelangelo Attardo Perinetti Casoni create exquisite icons in tempera and 24-carat gold leaf. Expensive? Yes. Worth it? You bet. (www.arteinsiena.it; Via di Stalloreggi 47; ⏰hours vary)

Wednesday Market MARKET

24 🅐 MAP P160, A1

Spreading around Fortezza Medicea and towards the Stadio Comunale, this is one of Tuscany's largest markets and is great for cheap clothing; food is also sold. (admission free; ⏰7.30am-2pm)

Worth a Trip 👀
Chianti

Split between the provinces of Florence and Siena, this photogenic wine region is criss-crossed by a picturesque network of provincial secondary roads, some unsealed. An easy drive from Florence, you'll see immaculately maintained vineyards and olive groves, honey-coloured stone farmhouses, dense forests, handsome Renaissance villas and imposing stone castles built by warlords in the Middle Ages.

Tourist office (📞0558 54 62 99, 0558 5 36 06; www.helloflorence.net; Piazza Matteotti 11, Greve in Chianti; 🕙10.30am-1.30pm late Mar–mid-Oct, to 6.30pm Easter-Aug)

🚗 **Car** Take the SR222 (Via Chiantigiana)

Badia e Passignano

Chianti doesn't get much more atmospheric than this 11th-century Benedictine Vallombrosan abbey run by the legendary Antinori wine-making dynasty. Head here to visit the historic church and abbey buildings, admire the views and taste Antinori wines in the *enoteca* or neighbouring Michelin-starred **Osteria di Passignano** (www.osteriadipassignano.com).

Antinori nel Chianti Classico

To reach this strikingly contemporary **cellar complex** (☑0552 35 97 00; www.antinorichianti classico.it; Via Cassia 133, Località Bargino; tours & tastings from **€35**; ☺10am-5pm Mon-Fri, to 5.30pm Sat & Sun winter, to 6.30pm Sat & Sun summer) motor uphill to the main building, built into the hillside. One-hour guided tours finish with a tasting of three Antinori wines in an all-glass room suspended above barrels in the cellar.

Castello di Brolio

Home to the aristocratic Ricasoli family, this 11th-century **wine estate** (☑0577 73 02 80; www.ricasoli.it; Località Madonna a Brolio; garden, chapel & crypt €5, museum €3, guided tours with tasting adult/teenager from €30/20; ☺10am-5.30pm mid-Mar–Oct) is the oldest in Italy. It opens its formal garden, panoramic terrace and small museum to day-trippers, along with an *osteria* and a *cantina*.

Castello di Ama

Centuries-old winemaking traditions meet cutting-edge contemporary art at this 12th-century agricultural estate. Think vineyards, winery, boutique hotel, restaurant and sculpture park. Book **tours** (☑0577 74 60 69; www.castellodiama.com; Località Ama; guided tours adult/under 16yr €25/free; ☺enoteca 10am-7pm, tours by appointment) in advance.

★ **Top Tips**

o If meat is your sin, include the foodie hilltop town of Panzano in Chianti – home to Tuscany's celebrity butcher Dario Cecchini – in your itinerary.

o Advance bookings are essential to visit Antinori nel Chianti Classico, Castello di Ama and the vineyards and cellar at Badia a Passignano.

✕ **Take a Break**

o Head to the picturesque hilltop village of **Volpaia** near Radda in Chianti to visit the *cantina* (wine cellar) of the Castello di Volpaia wine estate and break for lunch over a snack at **Bar Ucci** (www.bar-ucci.it) or traditional Tuscan at **Ristorante La Bottega** (www.labottegadivolpaia.it).

Worth a Trip 👀
San Gimignano

As you crest the hill coming from the east, the 14 towers of this walled hilltop town look like a medieval Manhattan. Originally an Etruscan village, San Gimignano became prosperous in the Middle Ages due to its location on the Via Francigena pilgrimage route. Many of its inhabitants died in the 1348 plague. Today, not even the plague would deter the swarms of summer day-trippers lured by the medieval streets and enchanting rural setting.

Tourist Office (📞0577 94 00 08; www.sangimignano.com; Piazza del Duomo 1; 🕐10am-1pm & 3-7pm Mar-Oct, 10am-1pm & 2-6pm Nov-Feb)

🚌 **Bus** To/from Florence (€6.80, 1¼ to two hours) Change in Poggibonsi.

🚗 **Car** Siena–Florence superstrada SR2 and SP1.

Collegiata

San Gimignano's Romanesque cathedral is known as the **Collegiata** (Duomo; Basilica di Santa Maria Assunta; ☎0577 28 63 00; www.duomosangimignano.it; Piazza del Duomo; adult/reduced €4/2; ⏰10am-7.30pm Mon-Fri, to 5.30pm Sat, 12.30-7.30pm Sun Apr-Oct, shorter hours Nov-Mar), a reference to the college of priests who originally managed it. Parts of the building date back to the second half of the 11th century, but its remarkably vivid frescoes, which resemble a vast medieval comic strip, date from the 14th century.

Palazzo Comunale

The 13th-century **Palazzo Comunale** (☎0577 28 63 00; www.sangimignanomusei.it; Piazza del Duomo 2; combined Civic Museums ticket adult/reduced €9/7; ⏰10am-7.30pm Apr-Sep, 11am-5.30pm Oct-Mar) has always been the centre of San Gimignano's local government; its magnificently frescoed Sala di Dante is where the great poet addressed the town's council in 1299 and its Camera del Podestà and Pinacoteca (Art Gallery) once housed government offices – now they are home to wonderful artworks. Be sure to climb the 218 steps of the *palazzo's* 54m **Torre Grossa** for a spectacular view over the town and surrounding countryside.

Galleria Continua

This commercial **art gallery** (☎0577 94 31 34; www.galleriacontinua.com; Via del Castello 11; admission free; ⏰10am-1pm & 2-7pm) – one of Europe's best – exhibits the work of big-name artists such as Ai Weiwei, Daniel Buren, Antony Gormley and Mona Hatoum. Spread over four venues (an old cinema, a medieval tower, a vaulted cellar and an apartment on Piazza della Cisterna), it's one of San Gimignano's most compelling attractions.

★ **Top Tips**

○ Ask at the tourist office about money-saving combined museum tickets; it also organises guided tours and takes booking for wine-tasting master classes in town.

○ Be sure to sample local white wine Vernaccia di San Gimignano.

✕ **Take a Break**

○ Try excellent pasta dishes and house Vernaccia at **Ristorante La Mandragola** (www.locandalamandragola.it).

○ Grab a *panino* with locally sourced ingredients at **Dal Bertelli** (via Capassi 30) and a gelato at **Gelateria Dondoli** (www.gelateria-dipiazza.com).

Worth a Trip San Gimignano

Survival Guide

Central Florence SKANDARAMANA/SHUTTERSTOCK ©

Before You Go

Book Your Stay

○ Accommodation options include hostels, family-run *pensioni* (guesthouses), B&Bs, boutique hotels and luxury villa or *palazzo* (palace) hotels. It is always wise to book well ahead.

○ Hotels are nonsmoking by national law and many offer accommodation for mobility-impaired guests.

○ Cities and towns charge a *tassa di soggiorno* (hotel occupancy tax) on top of advertised hotel rates. It is always charged in addition to your hotel bill and must generally be paid in cash. The exact amount, which varies from city to city, depends on how many spangly stars your hotel is endowed with and the time of year. Expect to pay €1.50 per person per night in a one-star hotel or hostel, €2.50 in a B&B, €1.50 to €3.50 in an *agriturismo* (farm stay), €3.50 in a

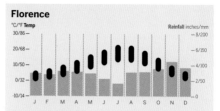

Florence

°C/°F Temp   Rainfall inches/mm

30/86 —   — 8/200

20/68 —   — 6/150

10/50 —   — 4/100

0/32 —   — 2/50

-10/14 —   — 0

J F M A M J J A S O N D

When to Go

○ **Spring** (April and May) The start of Florence's tourist season.

○ **Summer** (June to August) Peak tourist season – the city gets hot and crowded in July. Many restaurants close in August.

○ **Autumn and winter** (September to March) A mellow time of year to visit, with with extraordinary light.

three-star hotel and up to €5 in a four- or five-star hotel.

Useful Websites

Lonely Planet (lonely planet.com/italy/ florence/hotels) Recommendations.

Cross-Pollinate (www. cross-pollinate.com) Excellent source of guesthouses, B&Bs and self-catering apartments for all budgets, personally vetted by the folk behind Rome's highly recommended Beehive hostel.

Apartments Florence (www.apartments florence.it) Just that.

Homes in Florence (www.homesinflorence. it) Reliable reference point for self-catering apartments and family homes in and around Florence.

Lungarno Collection (www.lungarnocollec tion.com) Boutique collection of luxurious hotels owned by the Ferragamo fashion empire.

Wtb Hotels (www. whythebesthotels.com) Florence-based hotel group.

Best Budget

Academy Hostel (www.academyhostel. eu) Up-to-the-minute

hostel digs in San Lorenzo.

Hotel Scoti (www.hotelscoti.com) Great-value budget pensione in a frescoed *palazzo*.

Hotel Marine (www.hotelmarineflorence.com) No-frills hotel with stunning, rooftop breakfast terrace.

Hotel Dali (www.hoteldali.com) Family-run digs near the Duomo with free parking.

Best Midrange

Hotel Pendini (www.hotelpendini.it) Stylish midranger in the biz on Piazza della Repubblica since 1879.

Hotel Davanzati (www.davanzati.it) Charming address with charisma and five-star service.

Hotel Orto de' Medici (www.ortodeimedici.it) Enchanting garden hotel with period dress in San Marco.

Palazzo Belfiore (www.palazzobelfiore.it) Stylish, self-catering apartments on the Oltrarno.

Best Top End

Ad Astra (www.adastraflorence.com)

Chic designer guesthouse in a historic walled garden.

SoprArno Suites (www.sopranosuites.com) Bespoke, uber-stylish B&B in the Oltrarno.

Palazzo Vecchietti (www.palazzovecchietti.com) Buzzword for hotel chic, wedged between designer fashion boutiques.

Arriving in Florence & Tuscany

Florence Airport

○ Alternative names: Amerigo Vespucci; Peretola.

○ Volainbus shuttle buses (single/return €6/10, 30 minutes) travel to Piazza della Stazione every 30 minutes between 6am and 8.30pm, then hourly until 11.30pm.

○ A taxi to the *centro historico* (historical centre) costs a flat rate of €20 (€24 on Sundays and holidays, €25.30

between 10pm and 6am), plus €1 per bag.

Pisa International Airport

○ Alternative name: Aeroporto Galileo Galilei.

○ Tuscany's major air hub, linked with Florence's Stazione di Santa Maria Novella by train (€7.80, 1½ hours, at least hourly from 4.30am to 10.25pm).

○ Regular trains link Stazione di Santa Maria Novella with Pisa's central train station, Pisa Centrale (€9.70, 1½ hours, at least hourly from 4.30am to 10.25pm), from where the high-speed, fully automatic People Mover train (http://pisa-mover.com; €2.70, five minutes, every five minutes from 6am to midnight) continues to Pisa International Airport.

○ Hourly bus services to Stazione di Santa Maria Novella are operated by Terravision (www.terravision.eu; one way €4.99, 70 minutes) and Autostradale (www.airportbusexpress.it; single/return €7.50/13.50, 80 minutes, hourly). Buy tickets online or on board.

Stazione di Santa Maria Novella

◦ Most neighbourhoods are an easy walk from Florence's main train station, located on the northwestern edge of the historical centre.

Getting Around

Florence itself is small and best navigated on foot; most major sights are within easy walking distance.

Bicycle

◦ City bikes to rent in front of Stazione di Santa Maria Novella and elsewhere in the city.

Bus & Tram

◦ Buses to Fiesole (bus 7) leave from Piazza San Marco.

◦ Bus 13 runs uphill to Piazzale Michelangelo and Basilica di San Miniato al Monte. It leaves from the Autolinee Toscane bus stops near Stazione di Santa Maria Novella.

◦ Tickets are valid for 90 minutes and cost €1.20 at *tabacchi* (tobacco-

nists) or the Autolinee Toscane ticket and information office adjoining the train station, but cost €2 when purchased on board. A travel pass valid for 1/3 days is €5/12.

◦ Upon boarding, time stamp your ticket (punch on board) or risk a €50 fine.

◦ Buses to Siena and San Gimignano depart from the SITA bus station in Via Santa Caterina da Siena, off Piazza della Stazione.

Car & Motorcycle

◦ Nonresident traffic is banned from the historic centre; parking is an absolute headache and best avoided.

Taxi

◦ Can't be hailed on the street; find ranks at train and bus stations or call 055 42 42 or 055 43 90.

Train

◦ Frequent services to Pisa, and less frequent to Lucca; check arrival and departure details at www.trenitalia.com.

◦ Pisa and Lucca historical centres are an easy walk from their central train stations.

Essential Information

Business Hours

Opening hours vary throughout the year.

Banks 8.30am to 1.30pm and 3.30pm to 4.30pm Monday to Friday

Restaurants 12.30pm to 2.30pm and 7.30pm to 10pm

Cafes 7.30am to 8pm

Bars and pubs 10am to 1am

Shops 9am to 1pm and 3.30pm to 7.30pm (or 4pm to 8pm) Monday to Saturday, 11am to 7pm Sunday

Discount Cards

The **Firenze Card** (€72; www.firenzecard. it) is valid for 72 hours and covers admission to some 72 museums, villas and gardens in Florence, as well as unlimited use of public transport and free wi-fi across the city. It reduces queueing time in high season – museums have a seperate queue for card-holders. Buy online or in Florence at tourist offices or ticketing desks of participating museums. For EU citizens, the card covers those under 18 travelling with the card holder.

Electricity

230V/50Hz

230V/50Hz

Emergency & Important Numbers

Italy's country code	☎ 39
International access code	☎ 00
Ambulance	☎ 118
Police	☎ 113
Pan-European emergency; emergency from mobile phone	☎ 112

Money

ATMs Bancomats (ATMs) are widely available throughout Tuscany; the best way to obtain local currency.

Credit Cards International credit and debit cards can be used at any bancomat displaying the appropriate sign. Cards are also good for most hotels, restaurants, shops, supermarkets and motorway tollbooths.

Tipping Locals don't tip waiters, but most visitors leave 10% to 15%. Bellhops usually expect €1 to €2 per bag.

Public Holidays

New Year's Day (Capodanno or Anno Nuovo) 1 January

Epiphany (Epifania or Befana) 6 January

Easter Sunday (Domenica di Pasqua) March/April

Easter Monday (Pasquetta or Lunedì dell'Angelo) March/April

Liberation Day 25 April – marks the Allied

Cutting Queues

In high season, long queues are a fact of life at Florence's museums. But for a fee of €3 or €4 per ticket, tickets to nine museums including the Uffizi, Galleria dell'Accademia, Palazzo Pitti, Museo del Bargello and the Cappelle Medicee can be reserved.

In reality, the only museums where prebooking is vital are the Uffizi and Accademia – go online or call **Firenze Musei** (Florence Museums; ☎ 055 265 43 21; www.firenzemusei. it), with ticketing desks (open 8.30am to 7pm Tuesday to Sunday) at the Uffizi (p42) – go to Door 3 – and Palazzo Pitti (p116).

Victory in Italy, and the end of the German presence in 1945

Labour Day (Festa del Lavoro) 1 May

Republic Day (Festa della Repubblica) 2 June

Feast of the Assumption (Assunzione or Ferragosto) 15 August

All Saints' Day (Ognissanti) 1 November

Feast of the Immaculate Conception (Immaculata Concezione) 8 December

Christmas Day (Natale) 25 December

Boxing Day (Festa di Santo Stefano) 26 December

Telephone

○ Italy uses GSM 900/1800, compatible with the rest of Europe and Australia but not with North American GSM 1900 or the Japanese system.

Toilets

Public toilets are nonexistent, hence the perpetual queue at the public toilets inside department store La Rinascente on Piazza della Repubblica.

○ When the urge strikes, nip into the nearest cafe, order an espresso at the bar and consider the cost of €1 the price for using their facilities.

Tourist Information

Find tourist offices at both Florence and Pisa airports. In Florence, there are offices on Piazza della Stazione, opposite the train station; and in the Loggia del Bigallo, opposite the Duomo.

○ For tourist information check Visit Tuscany (www.visittuscany.com), Firenze Turismo (www.firenzeturismo.it), Pisa Tourism (www.pisa unicaterra.it), Il Blog di Lucca (www.luccatourist.it) for Lucca and Terre di Siena (www.terresiena.it) for Siena and San Gimignano.

Visas

○ European citizens of the 26 countries in the Schengen Area can enter Italy with nothing more than a valid identity card or passport.

○ Residents of some 28 non-EU countries, including the UK, Australia, Brazil, Canada, Israel, Japan, New Zealand and the USA, don't require visas for tourist visits of up to 90 days.

○ All non-EU and non-Schengen nationals entering Italy for more than 90 days, or for any reason other than tourism (such as study or work), may need a specific visa. For details, visit www.esteri.it or contact an Italian consulate.

○ Entry rules concerning COVID-19 vaccinations and testing requirements are changing frequently at the time of writing. Since mid-December 2021 all visitors, irrespective of vaccination status and departure destination, require proof of negative PCR (within 48 hours prior to arrival) or lateral-flow (antigen; within 24 hours) test to enter Italy. When planning your trip, check current rules and requirements carefully on Italy's Ministry of Health website (https://www.salute.gov.it) and carry out another 'play safe' check prior to departure for last-minute changes.

Dos & Don'ts

Greetings Shake hands and say *buongiorno* (good morning) or *buona-sera* (good afternoon/evening). If you know someone well, kissing both cheeks (starting with their left) is standard.

Polite language Say *mi scusi* to attract attention or say 'I'm sorry', *grazie (mille)* to say 'thank you (very much)', *per favore* to say 'please', *prego* to say 'you're welcome' or 'please, after you' and *permesso* if you need to push past someone in a crowd.

Body language Be wary of making a circle with two hands (which in Italy means 'I'll kick your ass'), an A-OK signal ('You might be gay') or the devil horns with your hand ('Your wife is cheating on you').

In churches Never intrude on a mass or service.

Selfie sticks Officially banned in Florentine museums.

Smoking Banned in enclosed public spaces; indulged in with gusto on many open-air cafe pavement terraces.

Responsible Travel

Overtourism

o Travel in low season: November to March is a rewarding time to visit cities and towns. In the Tuscan country-side, autumn raises the curtain on a banquet of zero-kilometre, culinary forest riches.

o In Florence, Pisa and Siena, don't dash in and out in a day. Stay longer to explore beyond the main sights and over-crowded city centre.

o Stay in registered accommodation. Favour local businesses like Your Place in Florence (www.yourplaceinflorence.com) to ensure a more personalised service and that your money remains in the local community.

o Embrace the sustain-able Uffizi Diffusi project: to spread the tourist load, the world-class gallery (p42) regularly displaces masterpieces to uncon-ventional pop-up venues in less-trodden parts of Florence and Tuscany.

o Consult Feel Florence (www.feelflorence.it) and download the Feel Florence app to unlock themed DIY walking, cycling and jogging tours in Florentine neighbour-hoods you most likely have never heard of.

Leave a light footprint

Explore Florence on foot or by bicycle, using its 90km of dedicated cycling lanes. Download the Movi by Mobile app to locate an electric bike by RideMovi (www.ridemovi.com). The city also has public-sharing kick scooters (www.timove.it and www.bitmobility.it), e-scooters (https://mimoto.it), cars (https://enjoy.eni.com) and electric cars (www.addumacars.it).

Language

Regional dialects are an important part of identity in many parts of Italy, but you'll have no trouble being understood anywhere if you stick to standard Italian, which is what we've also used in this chapter.

The sounds used in Italian can all be found in English. If you read our pronunciation guides as if they were English, you'll be understood. The stressed syllables are indicated with italics. Note that *ai* is pronounced as in 'aisle', *ay* as in 'say', *ow* as in 'how', *dz* as the 'ds' in 'lids', and that *r* is a strong and rolled sound.

To enhance your trip with a phrasebook, visit lonelyplanet.com.

Basics

Hello.
Buongiorno.   bwon·*jor*·no

Goodbye.
Arrivederci.   a·ree·ve·*der*·chee

How are you?
Come sta?   *ko*·me sta

Fine. And you?
Bene. E Lei?   *be*·ne e lay

Please.
Per favore.   per fa·*vo*·re

Thank you.
Grazie.   *gra*·tsye

Excuse me.
Mi scusi.   mee *skoo*·zee

Sorry.
Mi dispiace.   mee dees·*pya*·che

Yes./No.
Sì./No.   see/no

I don't understand.
Non capisco.   non ka·*pee*·sko

Do you speak English?
Parla inglese?   *par*·la een·*gle*·ze

Eating & Drinking

I'd like ...   *Vorrei ...*   vo·*ray* ..
  a coffee   *un caffè*   oon ka·*fe*
  a table   *un tavolo*   oon *ta*·vo·lo
  the menu   *il menù*   eel me·*noo*
  two beers   *due birre*   doo·e *bee*·re

What would you recommend?
Cosa mi   *ko*·za mee
consiglia?   kon·*see*·lya

Enjoy the meal!
Buon appetito!   bwon a·pe·*tee*·to

That was delicious!
Era squisito!   *e*·ra skwee·*zee*·to

Cheers!
Salute!   sa·*loo*·te

Please bring the bill.
Mi porta il   mee *por*·ta eel
conto, per favore? *kon* to per fa·*vo*·re

Shopping

I'd like to buy ...
Vorrei comprare ... vo·*ray* kom·*pra*·re ...

I'm just looking.
Sto solo   sto *so*·lo
guardando.   gwar·*dan*·do

How much is this?
Quanto costa questo? — kwan·to kos·ta kwe·sto

It's too expensive.
È troppo caro/cara. (m/f) — e tro·po ka·ro/ka·ra

Emergencies

Help!
Aiuto! — a·yoo·to

Call the police!
Chiami la polizia! — kya·mee la po·lee·tsee·a

Call a doctor!
Chiami un medico! — kya·mee oon me·dee·ko

I'm sick.
Mi sento male. — mee sen·to ma·le

I'm lost.
Mi sono perso/persa. (m/f) — mee so·no per·so/per·sa

Where are the toilets?
Dove sono i gabinetti? — do·ve so·no ee ga·bee·ne·tee

Time & Numbers

What time is it?
Che ora è? — ke o·ra e

It's (two) o'clock.
Sono le (due). — so·no le (doo·e)

1	*uno*	oo·no
2	*due*	doo·e
3	*tre*	tre
4	*quattro*	kwa·tro
5	*cinque*	cheen·kwe
6	*sei*	say
7	*sette*	se·te
8	*otto*	o·to
9	*nove*	no·ve
10	*dieci*	dye·chee
100	*cento*	chen·to
1000	*mille*	mee·le

Transport & Directions

Where's ...?
Dov'è ...? — do·ve ...

What's the address?
Qual è l'indirizzo? — kwa·le leen·dee·ree·tso

Can you show me (on the map)?
Può mostrarmi (sulla pianta)? — pwo mos·trar·mee (soo·la pyan·ta)

At what time does the ... leave?
A che ora parte ...? — a ke o·ra par·te

Does it stop at ...?
Si ferma a ...? — see fer·ma a ...

How do I get there?
Come ci si arriva? — ko·me chee see a·ree·va

morning	*mattina*	ma·tee·na
afternoon	*pomeriggio*	po·me·ree·jo
evening	*sera*	se·ra
yesterday	*ieri*	ye·ree
today	*oggi*	o·jee
tomorrow	*domani*	do·ma·nee
bus	*l'autobus*	low·to·boos
ticket	*un biglietto*	oon bee·lye·to
timetable	*orario*	o·ra·ryo
train	*il treno*	eel tre·no

Behind the Scenes

Send Us Your Feedback

We love to hear from travellers – your comments help make our books better. We read every word, and we guarantee that your feedback goes straight to the authors. Visit **lonelyplanet.com/contact** to submit your updates and suggestions.

Note: We may edit, reproduce and incorporate your comments in Lonely Planet products such as guidebooks, websites and digital products, so let us know if you don't want your comments reproduced or your name acknowledged. For a copy of our privacy policy visit lonelyplanet.com/privacy.

Acknowledgements

Cover photographs: Duomo and the Leaning Tower, Pisa, Ikonya/Getty Images ©, Tuscany, Stefano Termanini/Getty Images ©

Photographs pp30-1 (clockwise from top left): canadastock/Shutterstock ©, Petr Jilek/Shutterstock ©, OldskoolDesign/Shutterstock ©

Nicola's Thanks

Grazie mille to those who shared their love and insider knowledge: wine-tasting double-act Manuele Giovanelli and Zeno Fioravanti, Angela Banti, Doreen and Carmello, Georgette Jupe, serial foodie Coral Sisk, Nardia Plumridge, family tour guide and art historian Molly McIlwrath, Cailin Swanson and Betti Soldi, Caroline, Duccio di Giovanni and Marco Mantonavi. Finally, kudos to my very own expert, trilingual, family-travel research team: Niko, Mischa and Ka.

Virginia's Thanks

Many thanks to Tiziana Babbucci, Fernando Bardini, Maricla Bicci, Niccolò Bisconti, Enrico Bracciali, Rita Ceccarelli, Cecilia in Massa Marittima, Stefania Colombini, Ilaria Crescioli, Martina Dei, Paolo Demi, Federica Fantozzi, Irene Gavazzi, Francesco Gentile, Francesca Geppetti, Maria Guarriello, Benedetta Landi, Freya Middleton, Alessandra Molletti, Sonai Pallai, Luigi Pagnotta, Valentina De Pamphilis, Franco Rossi, Fabiana Sciano, Maria Luisa Scorza, Raffaella Senesi, Coral Sisk, Carolina Taddei and Luca Ventresa. Many thanks, too, to my travelling companions: Peter Handsaker, Eveline Zoutendijk, Max Handsaker, Elizabeth Maxwell, Matthew Clarke and Ella Clarke.

This Book

This 5th edition of Lonely Planet's *Pocket Florence & Tuscany* guidebook was curated by Nicola Williams, who researched and wrote it with Virginia Maxwell. This guidebook was produced by the following:

Destination Editor
Anna Tyler

Senior Product Editor
Amy Lynch

Product Editors Kate James, Jenna Myers, Alison Ridgway

Assisting Editors Sarah Bailey, James Bainbridge, Paul Harding, Jodie Martire, Anne Mulvaney, Kristin Odijk, Monique Perrin, Simon Williamson

Cartographers Anthony Phelan, Julie Sheridan

Book Designer Norma Brewer

Cover Researcher Brendan Dempsey-Spencer

Thanks to Sonia Kapoor

Index

See also separate subindexes for:

- Eating p187
- Drinking p188
- Entertainment p189
- Shopping p189